FOR ORGANS, PIANOS & ELECTRONIC KEYBOARDS

E-Z PLAY® TODAY

19

TOP COUNTRY SONGS

ISBN 978-1-4950-0090-4

HAL•LEONARD®
CORPORATION

7777 W. BLUEMOUND RD. P.O. BOX 13819 MILWAUKEE, WI 53213

Visit Hal Leonard Online at
www.halleonard.com

All I Want to Do

Registration 4
Rhythm: Country Pop or 8-Beat

Words and Music by Bobby Olen Pinson,
Kristian Bush and Jennifer Nettles

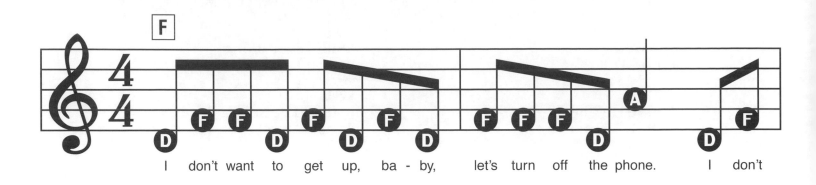

I don't want to get up, ba - by, let's turn off the phone. I don't

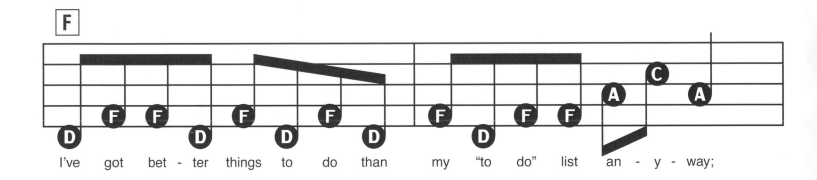

want to go to work to - day, or e - ven put my make - up on.

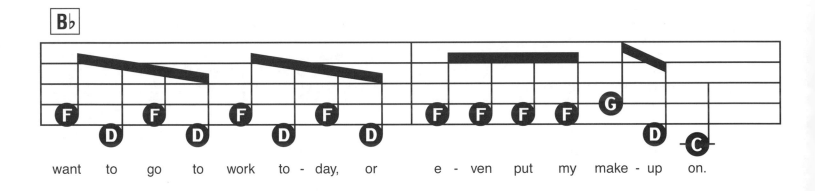

I've got bet - ter things to do than my "to do" list an - y - way;

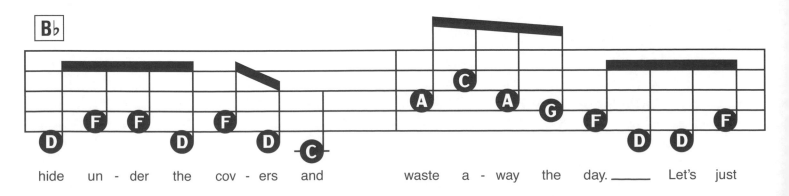

hide un - der the cov - ers and waste a - way the day. _____ Let's just

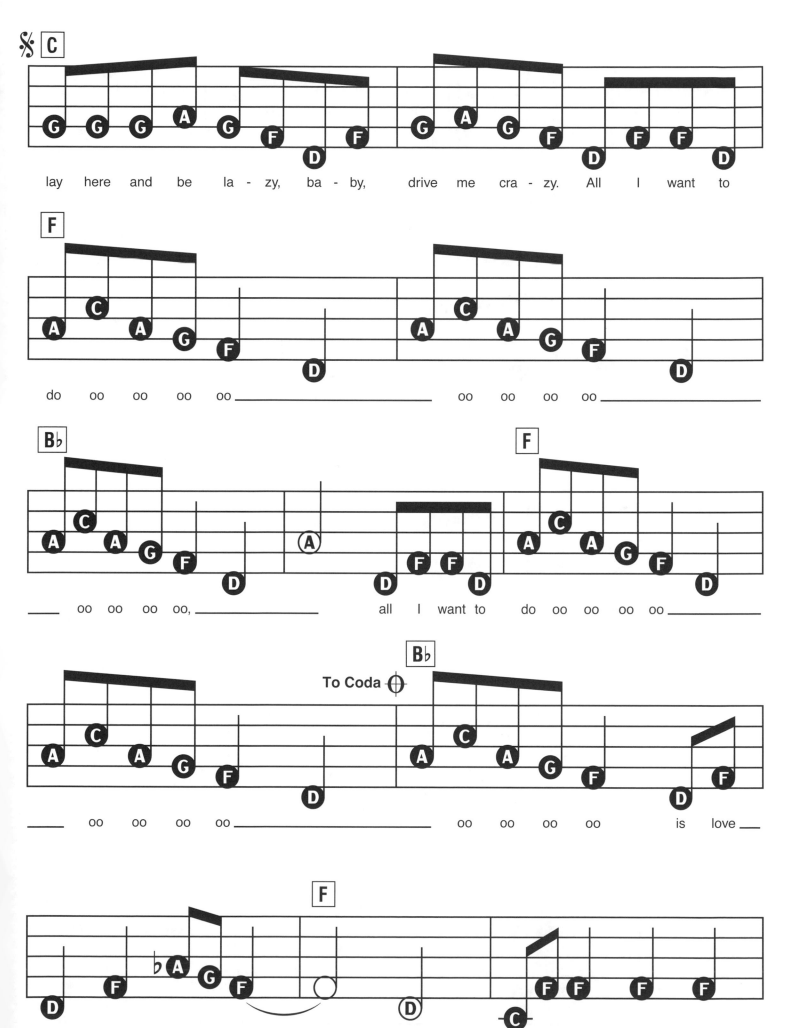

6

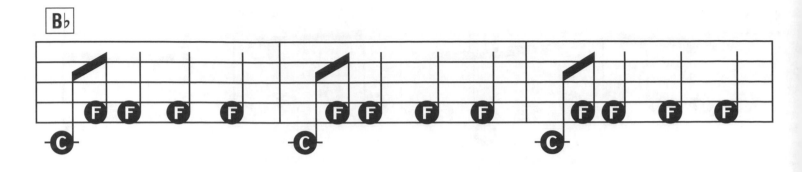

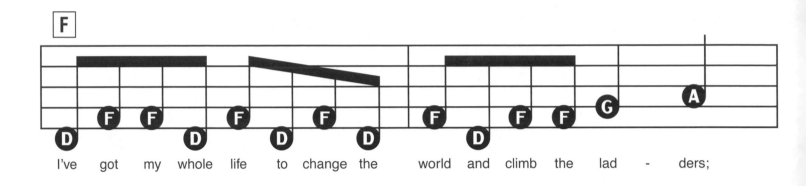

I've got my whole life to change the world and climb the lad - ders;

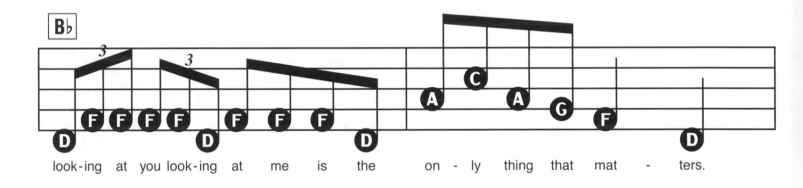

look-ing at you look-ing at me is the on - ly thing that mat - ters.

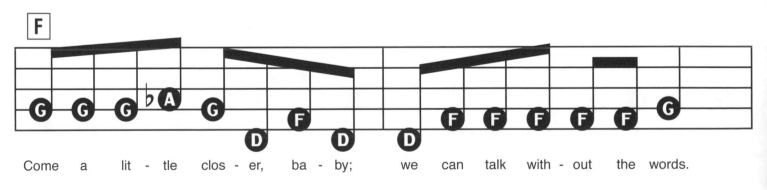

Come a lit - tle clos - er, ba - by; we can talk with - out the words.

D.S. al Coda
(Return to ℅
Play to ⊕ and
Skip to Coda)

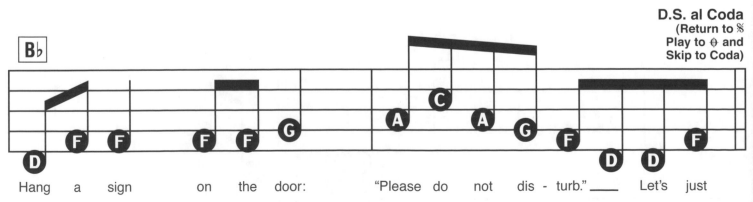

Hang a sign on the door: "Please do not dis - turb." ___ Let's just

CODA

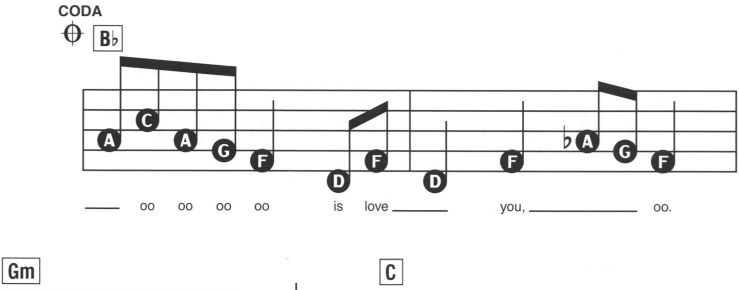

oo oo oo oo is love _____ you, _____ oo.

Give me a kiss from that El - vis lip.

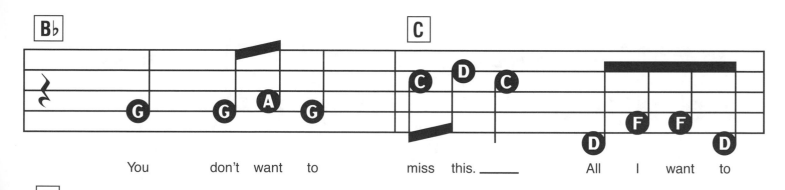

You don't want to miss this. _____ All I want to

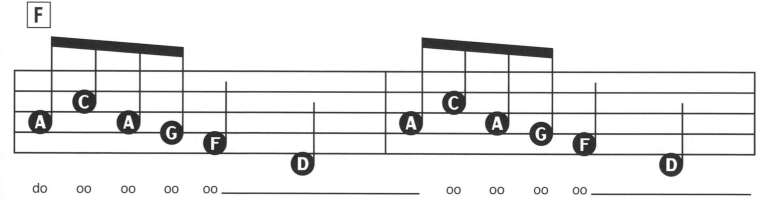

do oo oo oo oo _____ oo oo oo oo _____

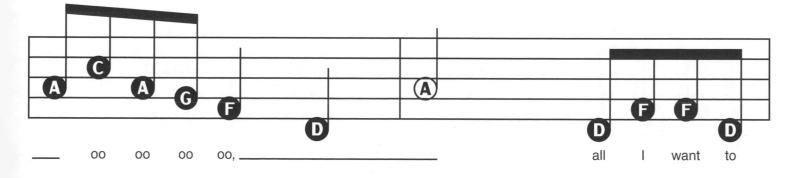

___ oo oo oo oo, _____ all I want to

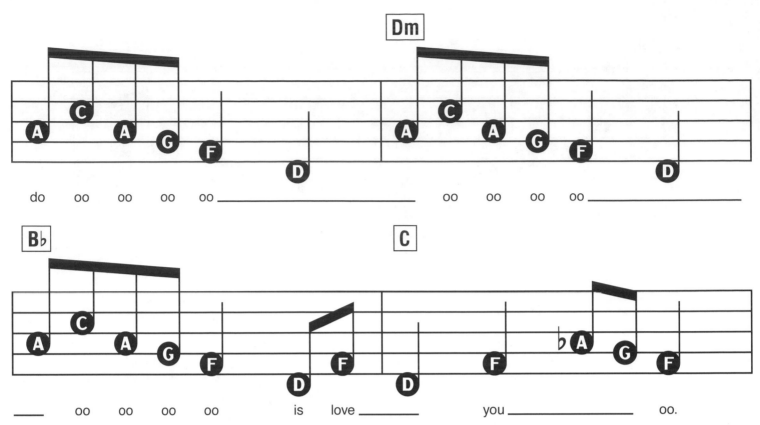

do oo oo oo oo _____ oo oo oo oo _____

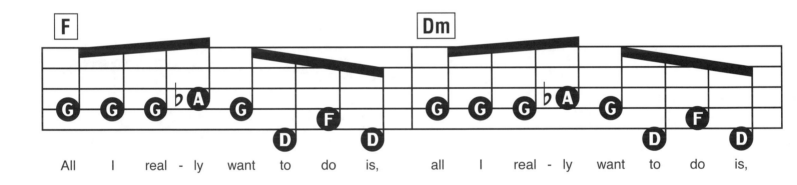

___ oo oo oo oo is love _____ you _____ oo.

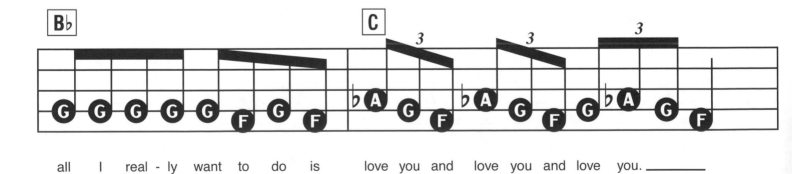

All I real - ly want to do is, all I real - ly want to do is,

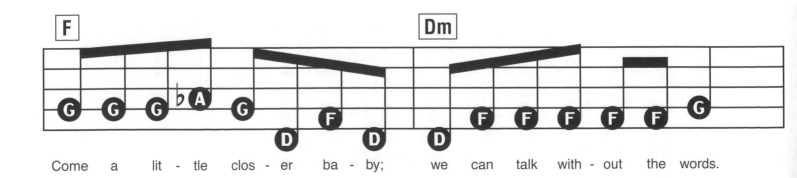

all I real - ly want to do is love you and love you and love you. _____

Come a lit - tle clos - er ba - by; we can talk with - out the words.

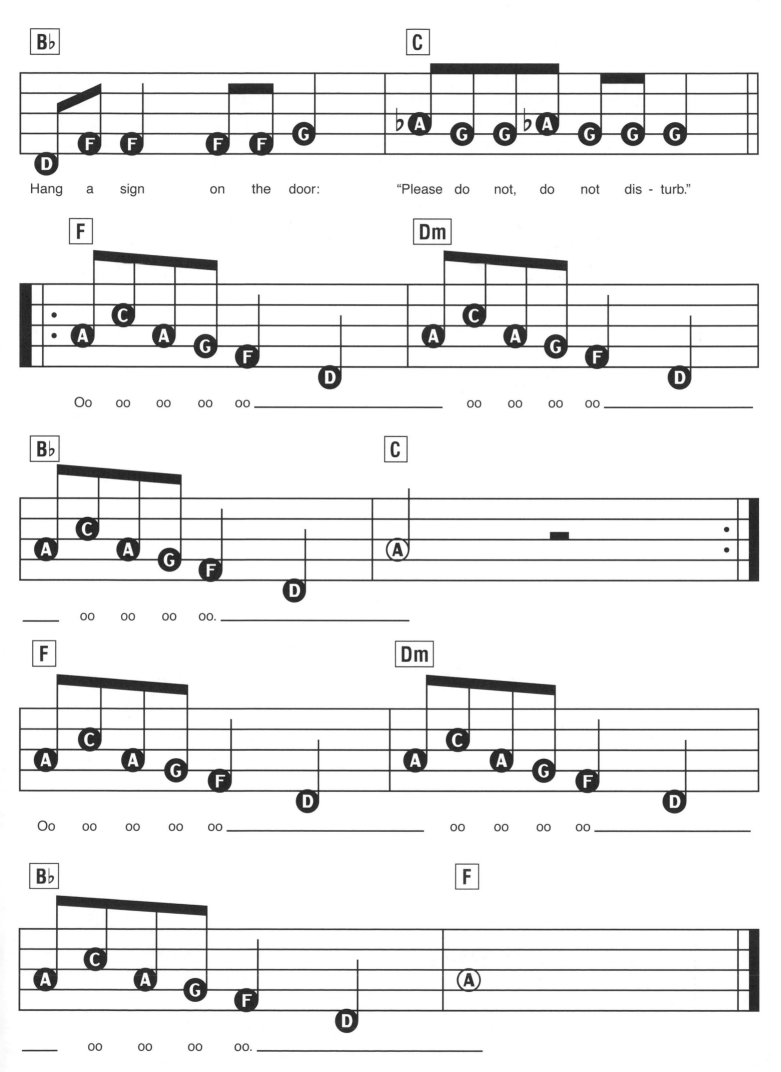

Hang   a   sign   on   the   door: "Please do   not,   do   not   dis - turb."

Oo   oo   oo   oo   oo _____   oo   oo   oo   oo _____

_____   oo   oo   oo   oo. _____

Oo   oo   oo   oo   oo _____   oo   oo   oo   oo _____

_____   oo   oo   oo   oo. _____

Amazed

Registration 3
Rhythm: Country

Words and Music by Marv Green,
Chris Lindsey and Aimee Mayo

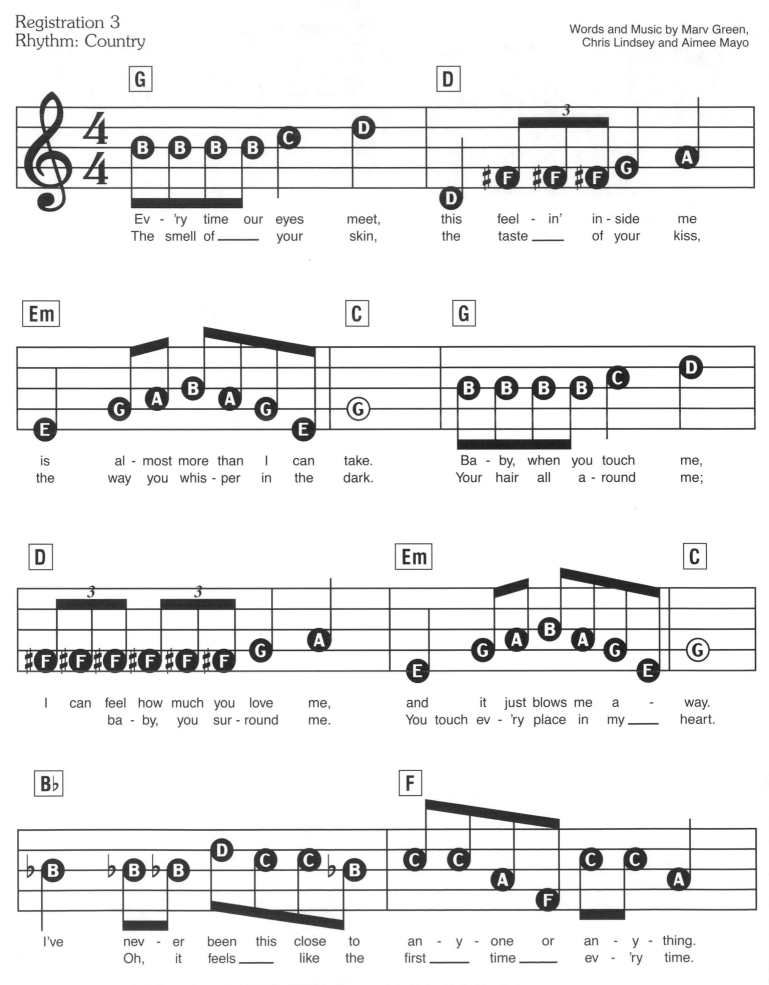

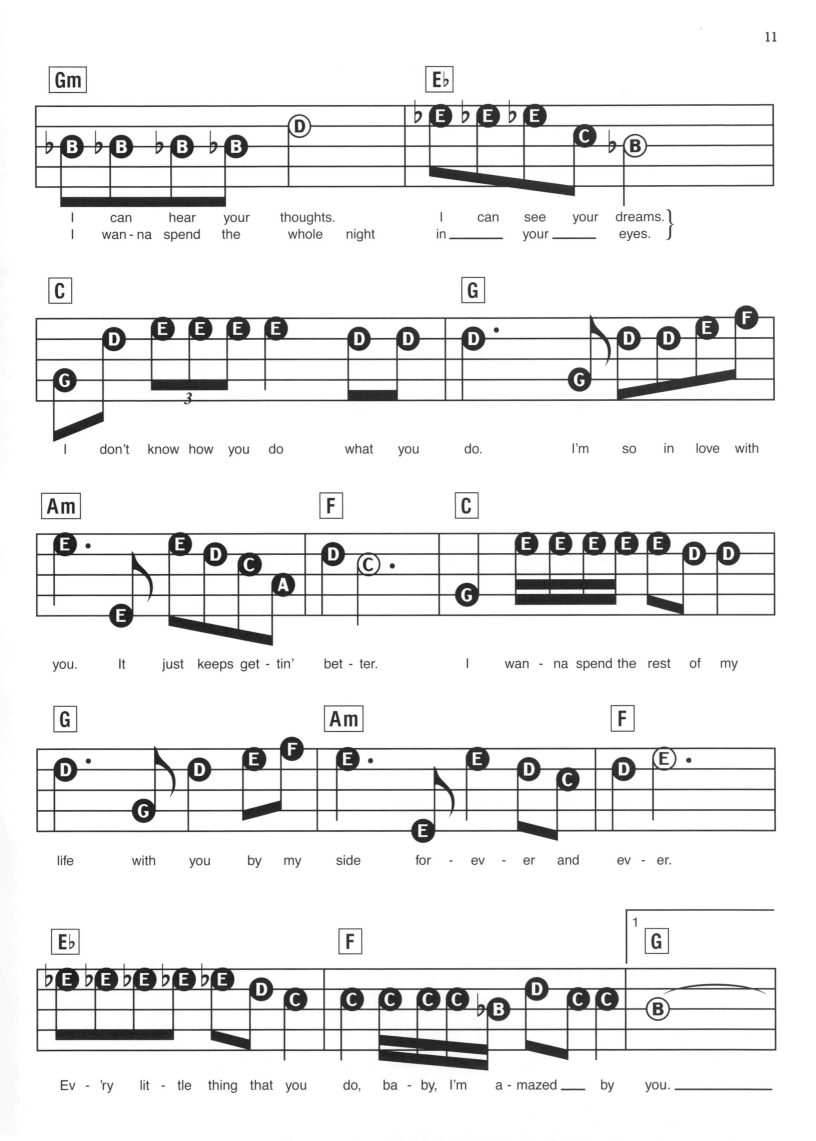

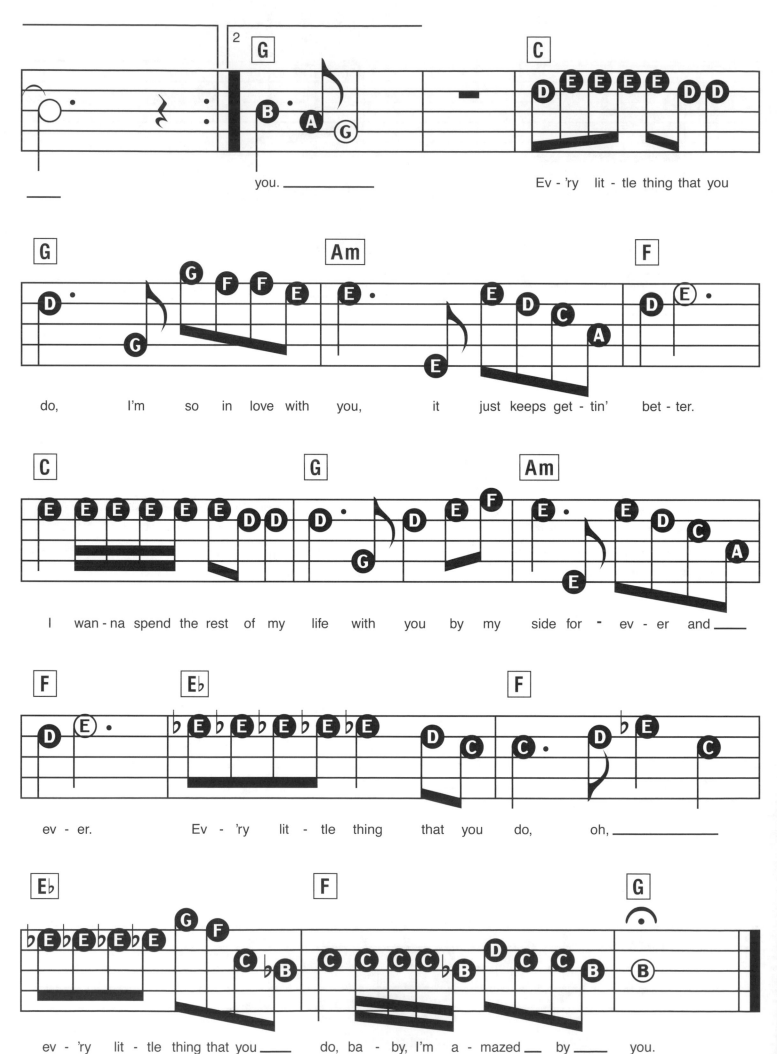

Before He Cheats

Registration 4
Rhythm: Country Rock or 8-Beat

Words and Music by Josh Kear
and Chris Tompkins

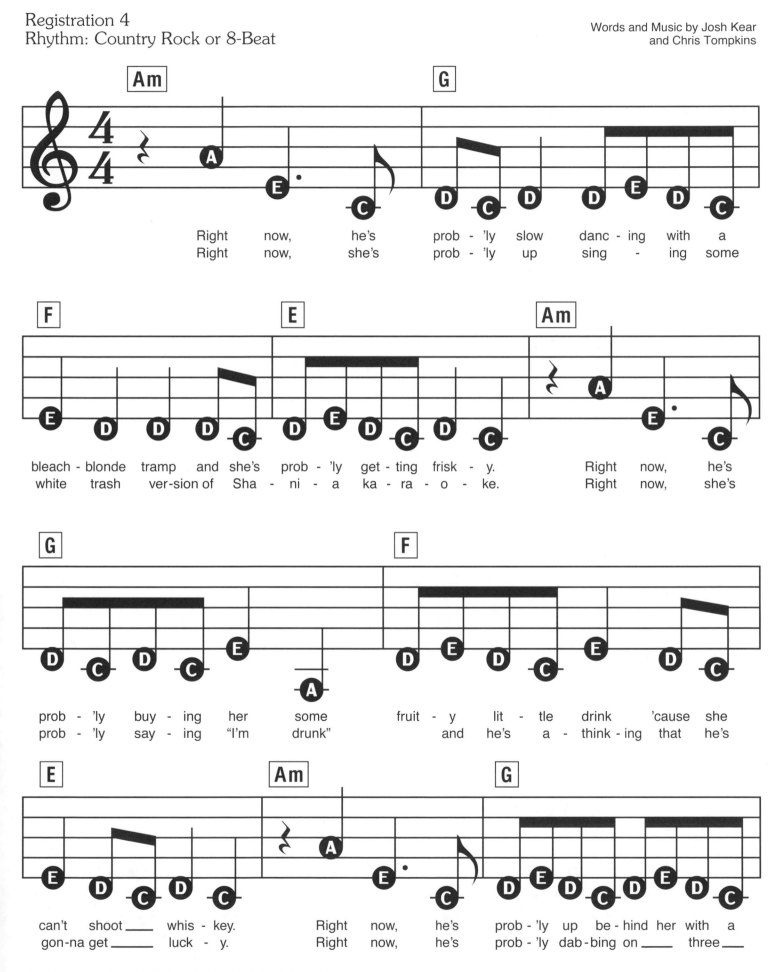

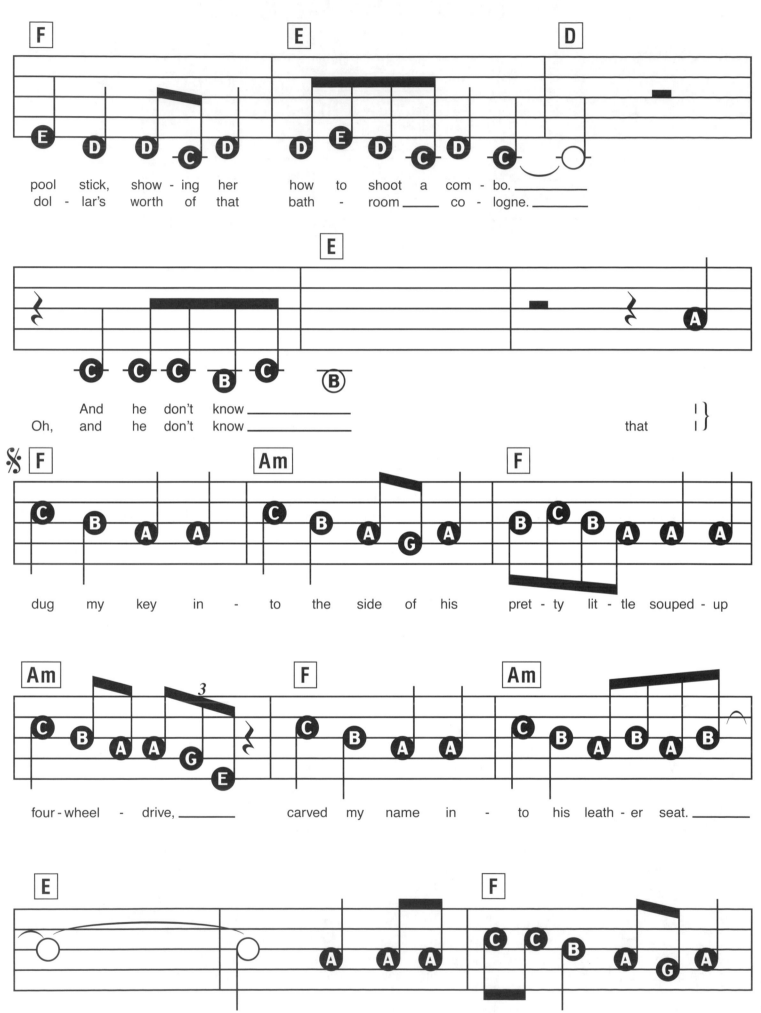

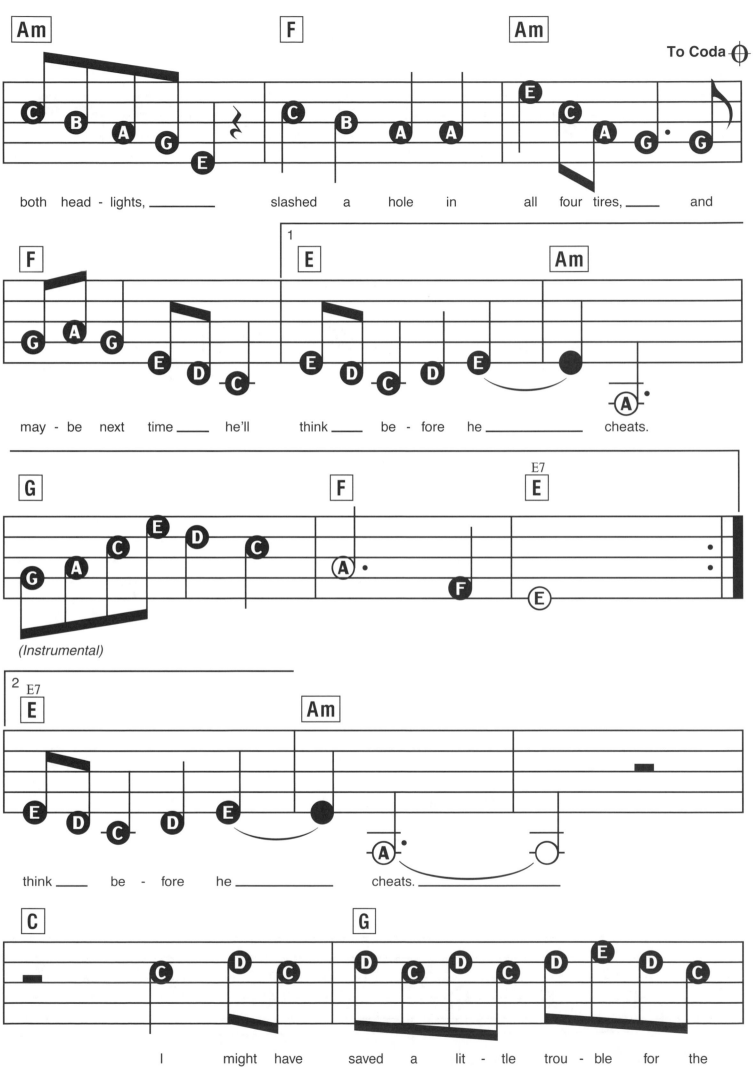

To Coda

both head - lights, _____ slashed a hole in all four tires, _____ and

1.

may - be next time _____ he'll think _____ be - fore he _____ cheats.

(Instrumental)

2.

think _____ be - fore he _____ cheats. _____

I might have saved a lit - tle trou - ble for the

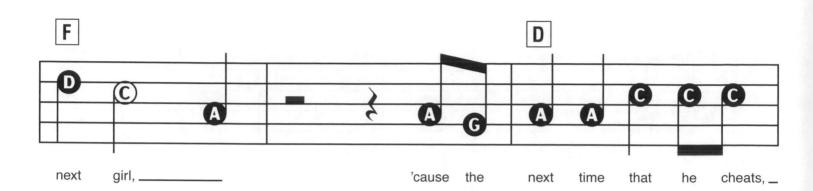

next girl, _____ 'cause the next time that he cheats, _

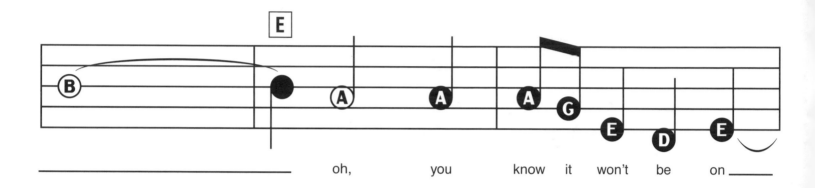

oh, you know it won't be on _____

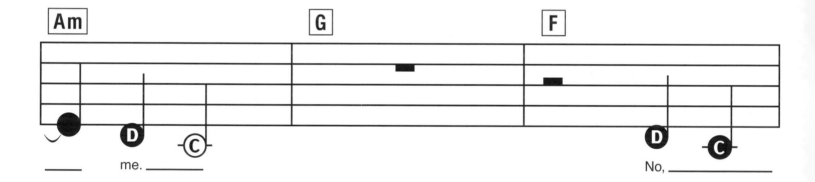

___ me. _____ No, _____

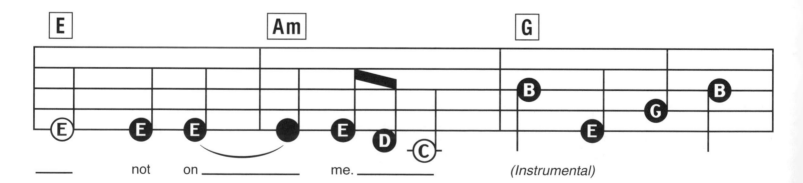

___ not on _____ me. _____ *(Instrumental)*

D.S. al Coda
(Return to %
Play to ⊕ and
Skip to Coda)

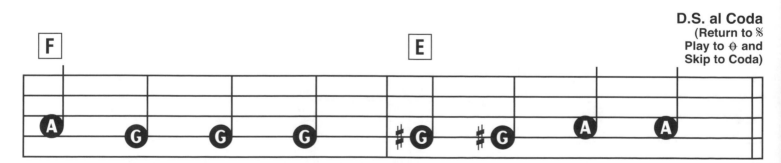

'Cause I

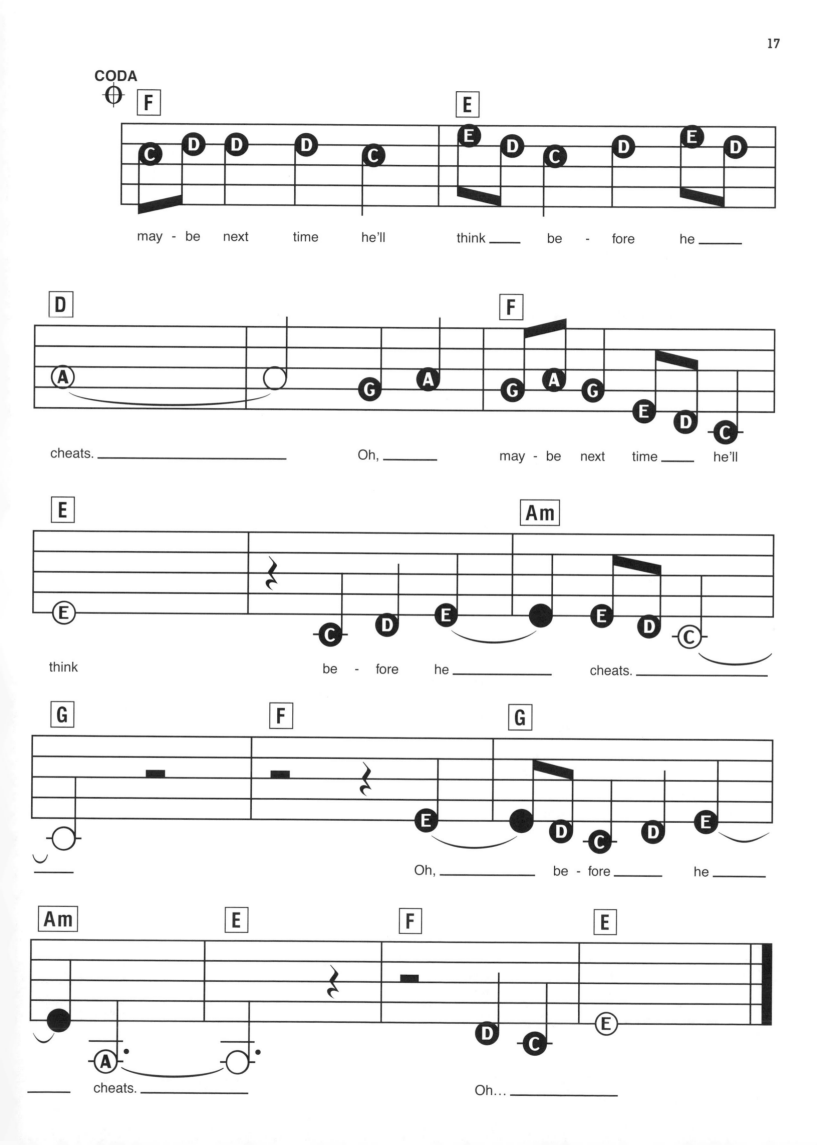

Cruise

Registration 4
Rhythm: Country Pop or Rock

Words and Music by Chase Rice,
Tyler Hubbard, Brian Kelley, Joey Moi
and Jesse Rice

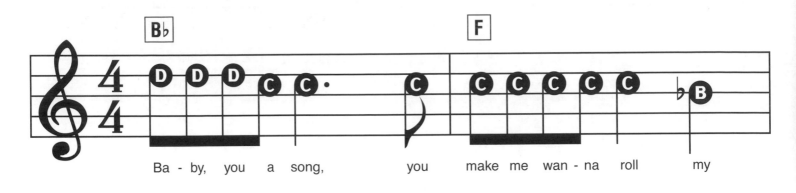

Ba - by, you a song, you make me wan - na roll my

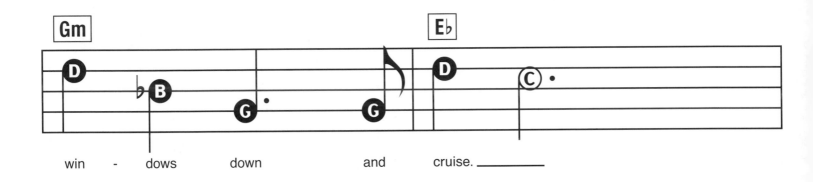

win - dows down and cruise. _____

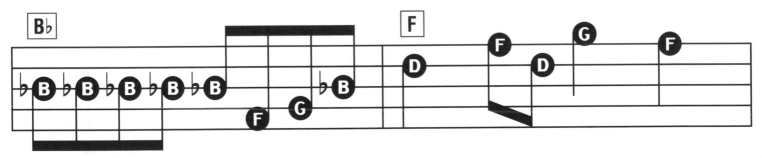

(Instrumental)

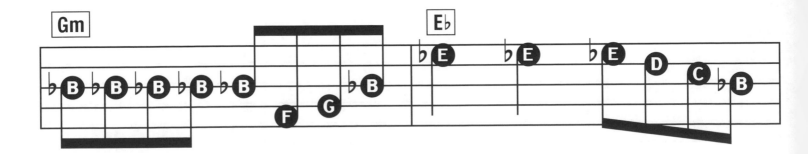

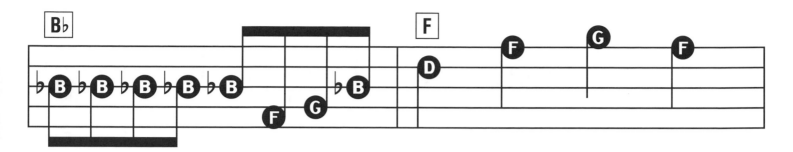

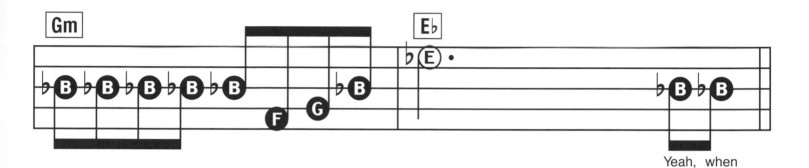

Yeah, when

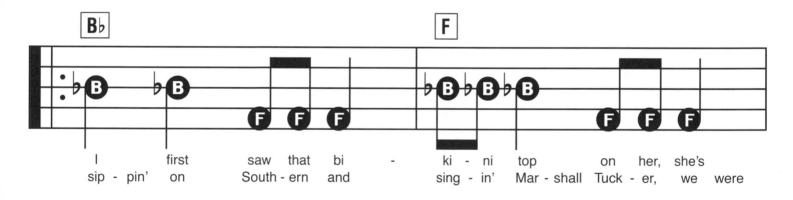

I first saw that bi - ki - ni top on her, she's
sip - pin' on South - ern and sing - in' Mar - shall Tuck - er, we were

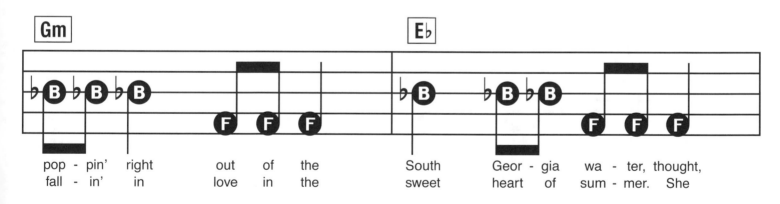

pop - pin' right out of the South Geor - gia wa - ter, thought,
fall - in' in love in the sweet heart of sum - mer. She

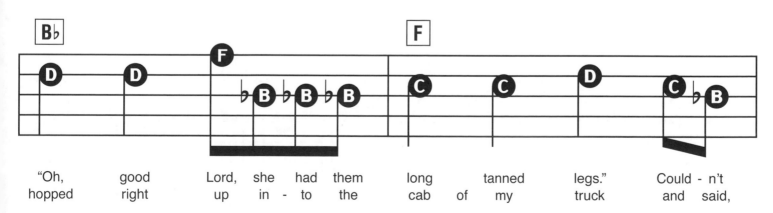

"Oh, good Lord, she had them long tanned legs." Could - n't
hopped right up in - to the cab of my truck and said,

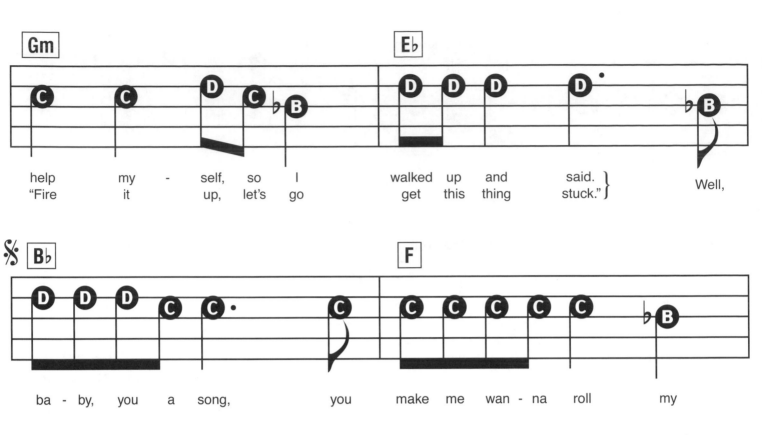

help my - self, so I walked up and said.
"Fire it up, let's go get this thing stuck." Well,

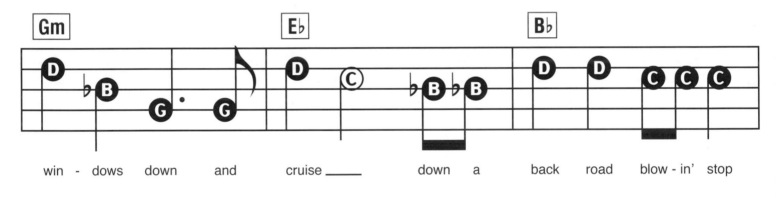

ba - by, you a song, you make me wan - na roll my

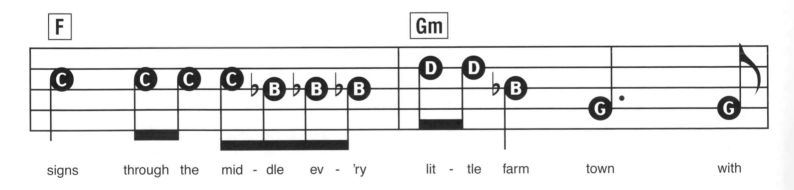

win - dows down and cruise _____ down a back road blow - in' stop

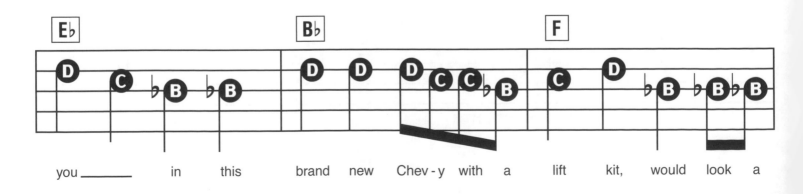

signs through the mid - dle ev - 'ry lit - tle farm town with

you _____ in this brand new Chev - y with a lift kit, would look a

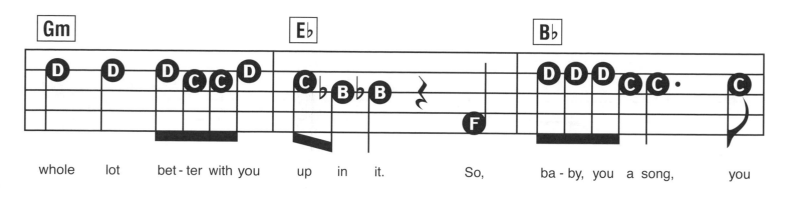

whole   lot   bet - ter with you   up   in   it.   So,   ba - by, you a song,   you

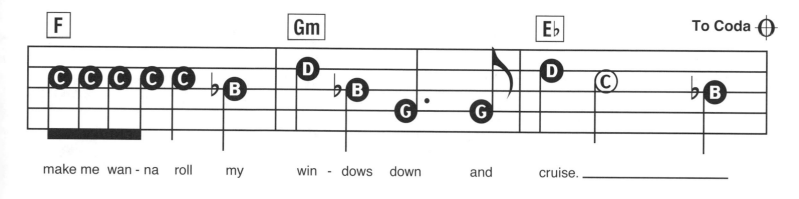

make me wan - na roll   my   win - dows down   and   cruise. _____

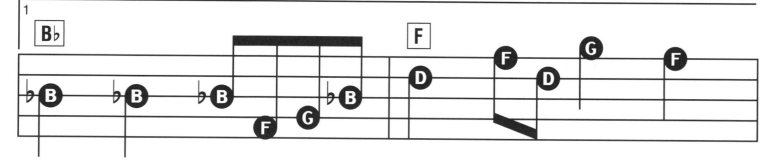

(Instrumental)

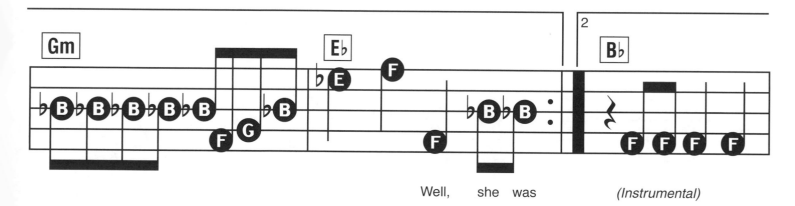

Well,   she was   *(Instrumental)*

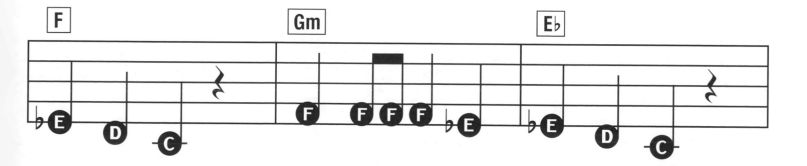

22

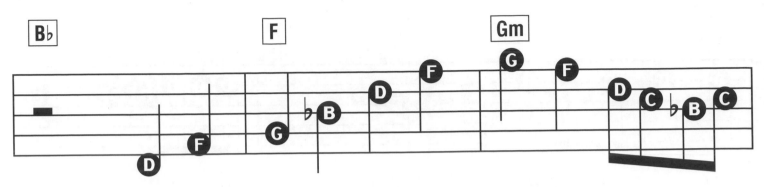

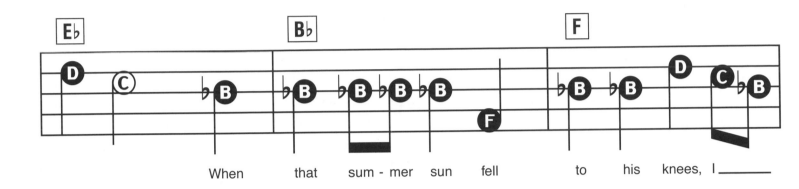

When that sum - mer sun fell to his knees, I ____

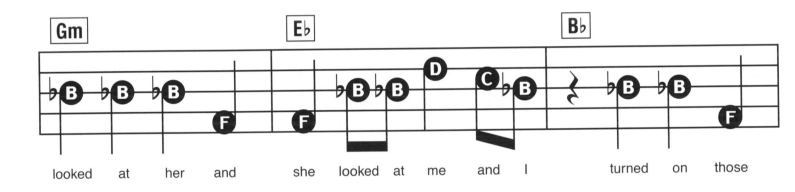

looked at her and she looked at me and I turned on those

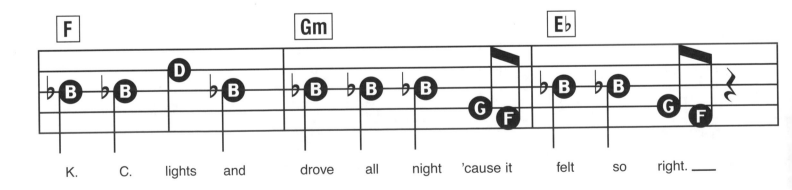

K. C. lights and drove all night 'cause it felt so right. ___

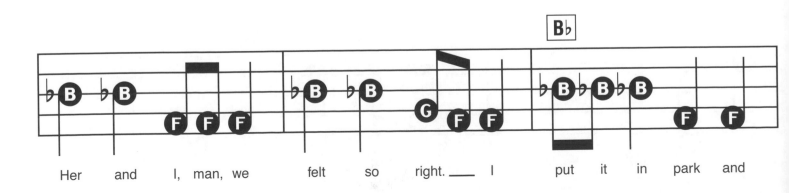

Her and I, man, we felt so right. ___ I put it in park and

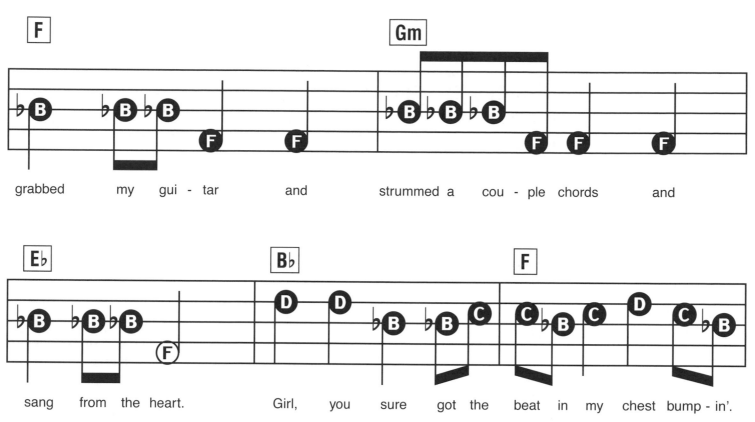

grabbed my gui - tar and strummed a cou - ple chords and

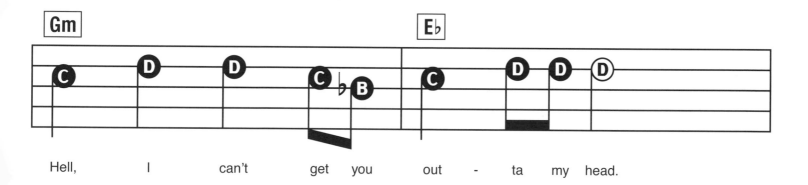

sang from the heart. Girl, you sure got the beat in my chest bump - in'.

Gm

Hell, I can't get you out - ta my head.

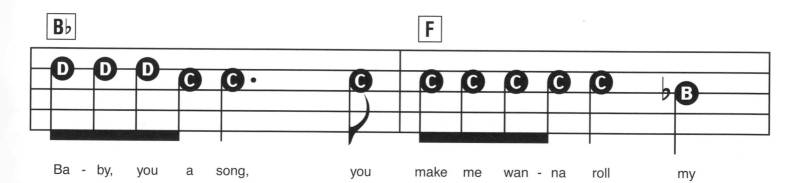

Ba - by, you a song, you make me wan - na roll my

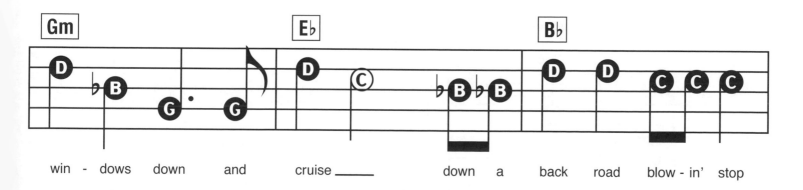

win - dows down and cruise _____ down a back road blow - in' stop

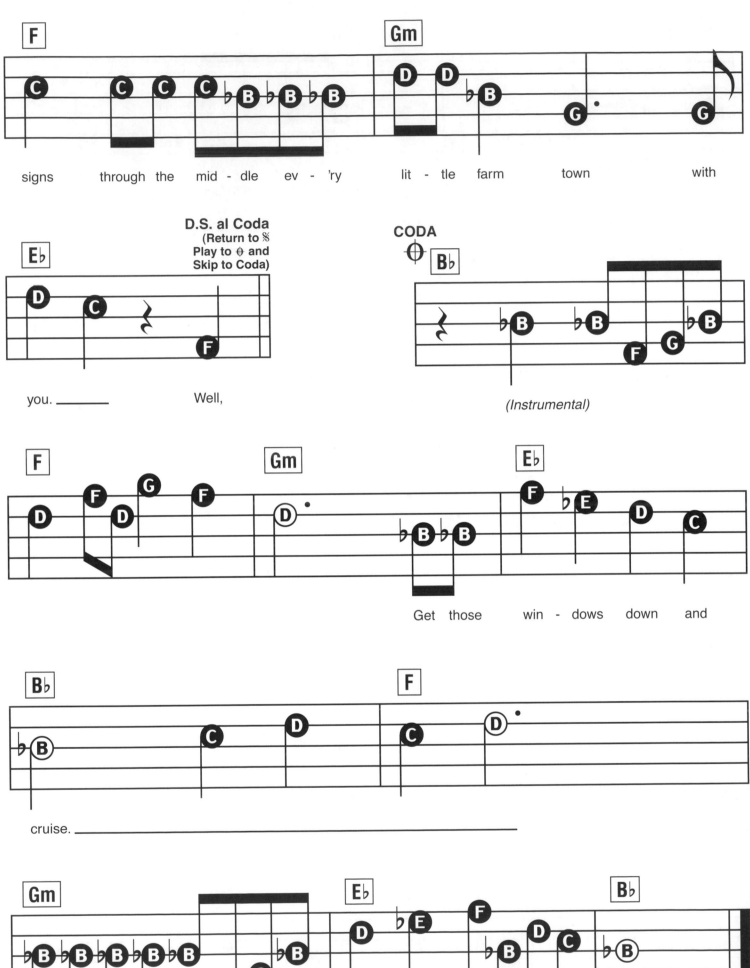

signs   through the   mid - dle   ev - 'ry   lit - tle   farm   town   with

D.S. al Coda
(Return to %
Play to ⊕ and
Skip to Coda)

CODA

you. _____   Well,

(Instrumental)

Get   those   win - dows   down   and

cruise. _____

(Instrumental)

Don't You Wanna Stay

Registration 4
Rhythm: Ballad or Country Pop

Words and Music by Jason Sellers,
Paul Jenkins and Andrew Gibson

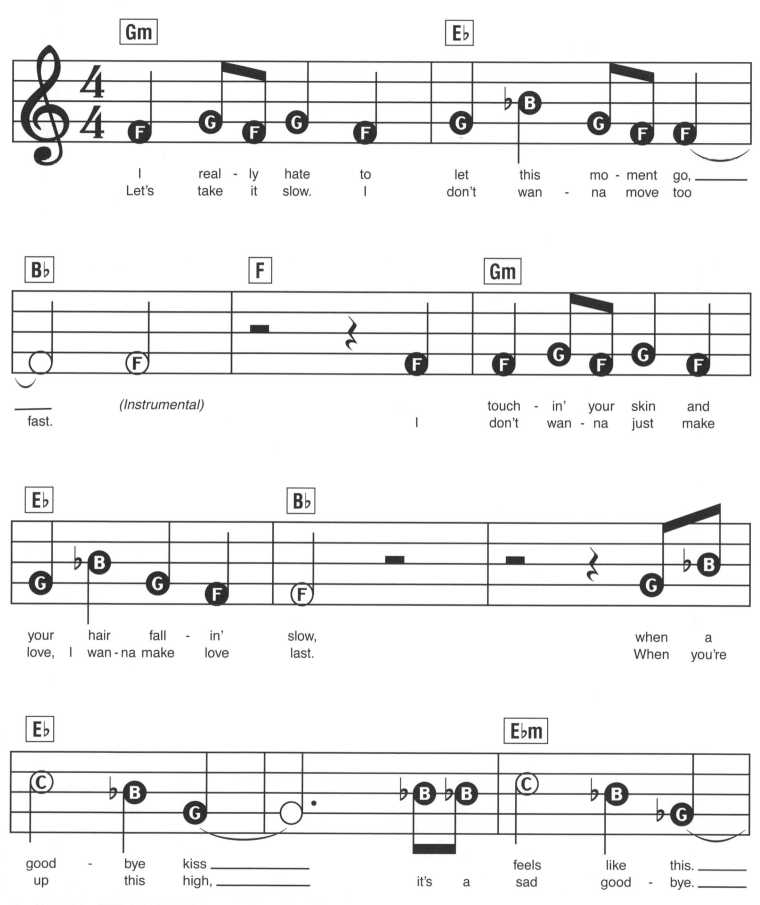

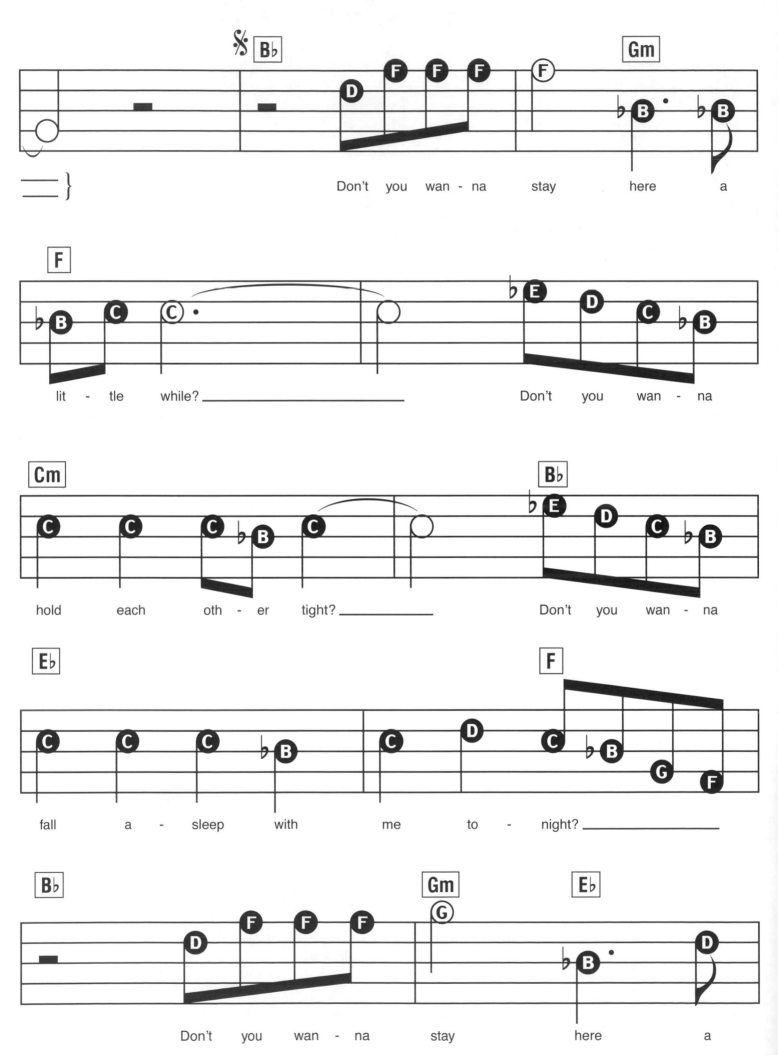

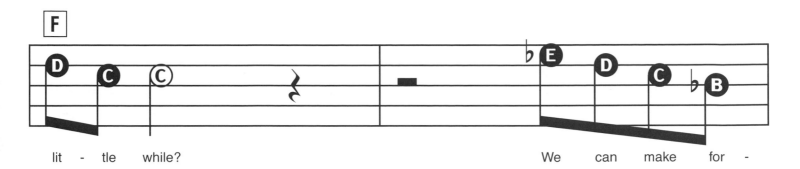

lit - tle while?   We can make for -

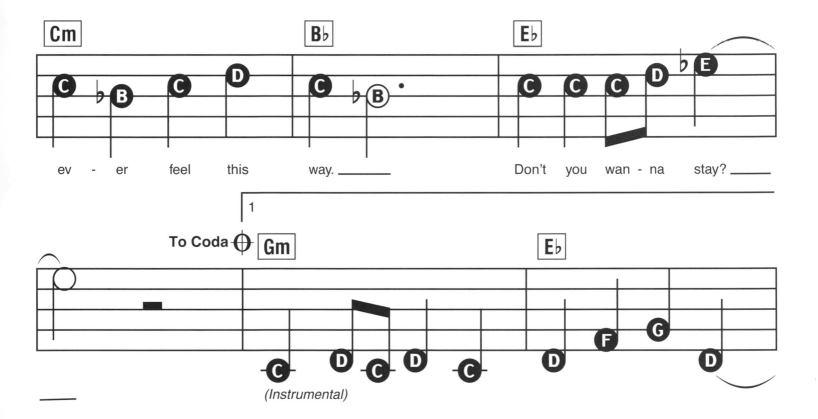

ev - er feel this   way. _____   Don't you wan - na stay? _____

(Instrumental)

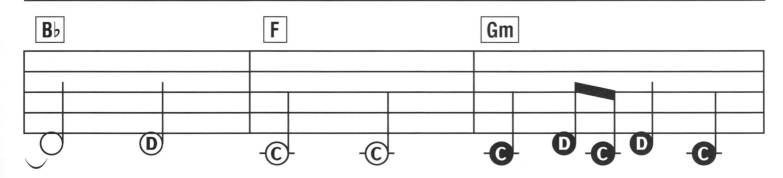

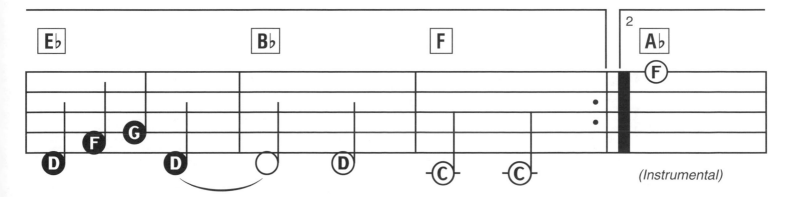

(Instrumental)

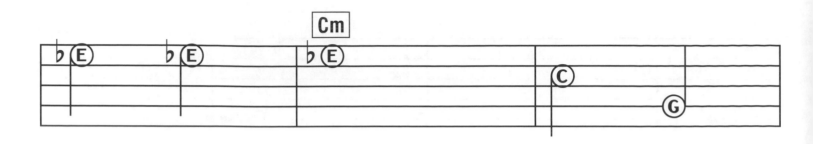

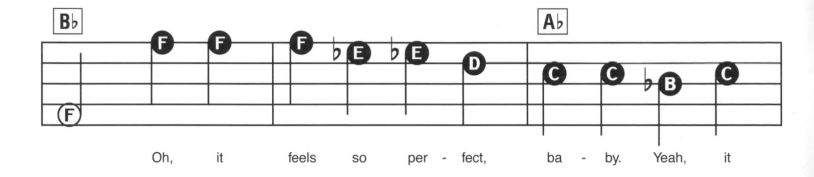

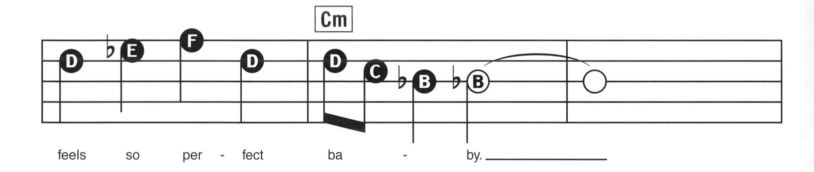

Oh, it feels so per - fect, ba - by. Yeah, it

feels so per - fect ba - by. _____

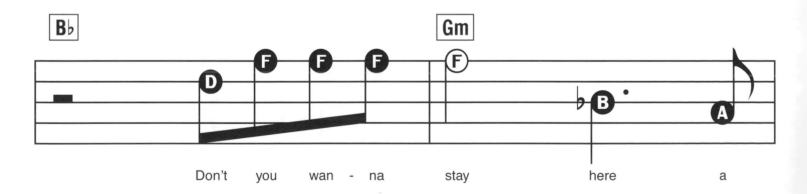

Don't you wan - na stay here a

D.S. al Coda
(Return to %
Play to ⊕ and
Skip to Coda)

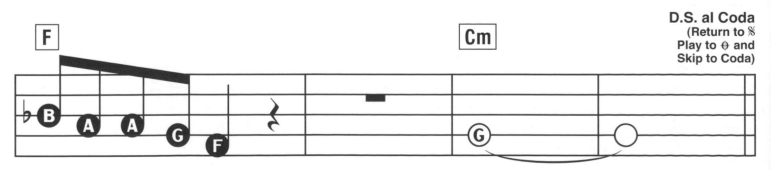

lit - tle while? _____

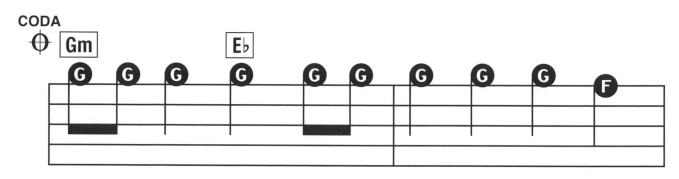

(Instrumental)

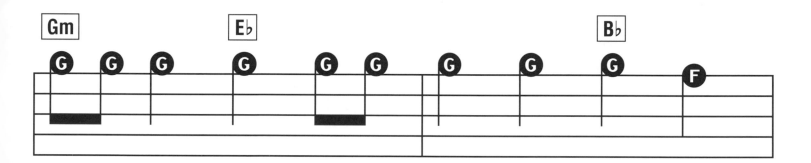

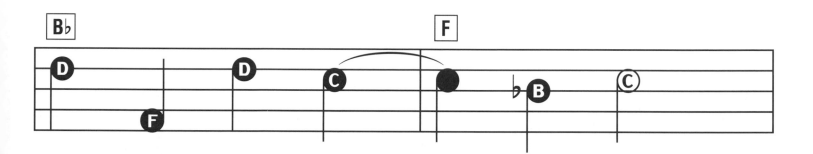

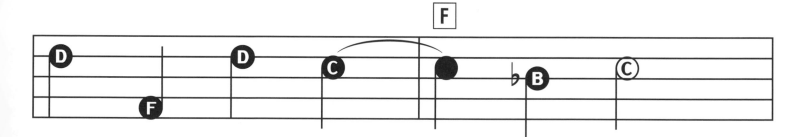

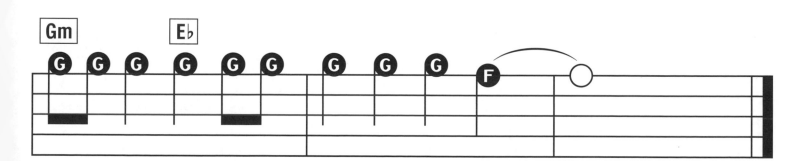

Farmer's Daughter

Registration 2
Rhythm: Country Rock or 8-Beat

Words and Music by Rhett Akins,
Ben Hayslip and Marv Green

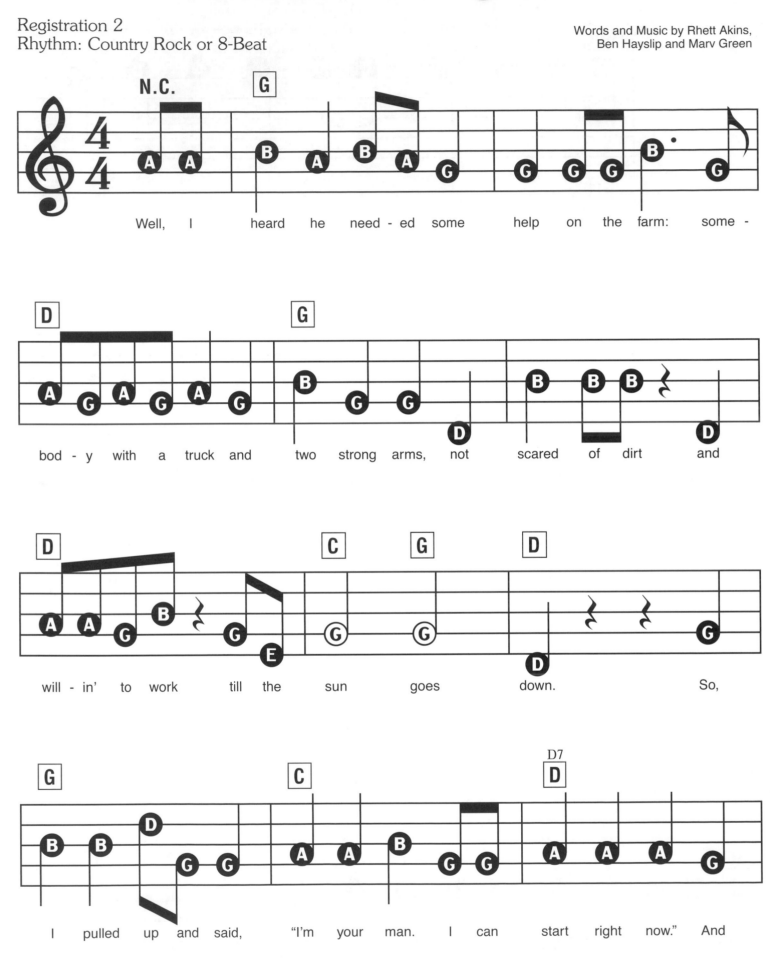

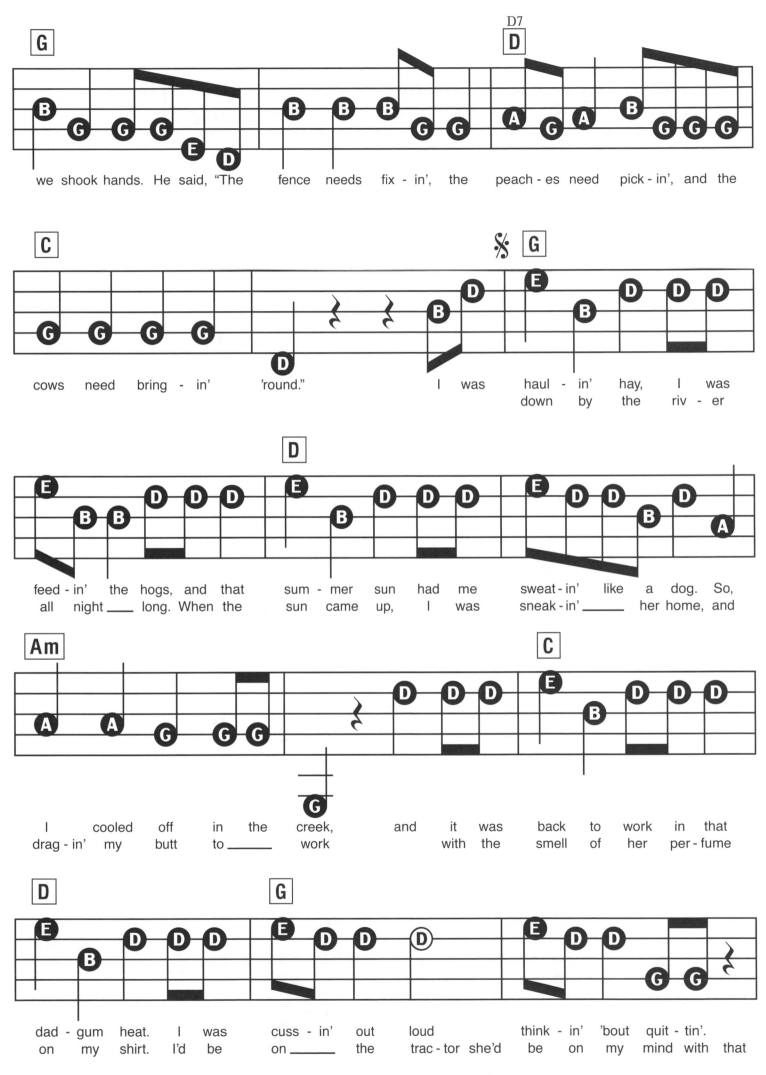

31

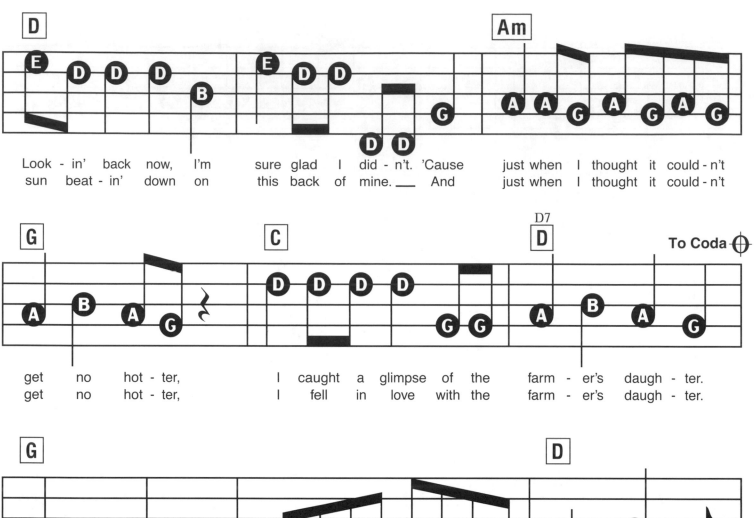

Look - in' back now, I'm sure glad I did - n't. 'Cause just when I thought it could - n't
sun beat - in' down on this back of mine. ___ And just when I thought it could - n't

get no hot - ter, I caught a glimpse of the farm - er's daugh - ter.
get no hot - ter, I fell in love with the farm - er's daugh - ter.

(Instrumental)

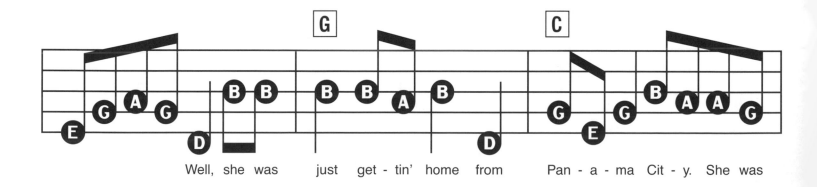

Well, she was just get - tin' home from Pan - a - ma Cit - y. She was

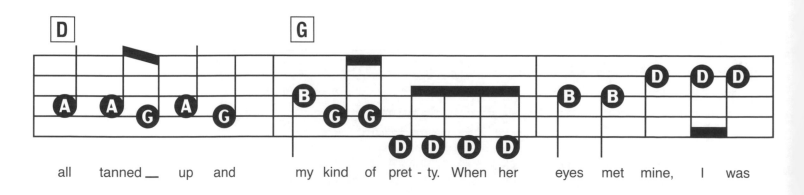

all tanned ___ up and my kind of pret - ty. When her eyes met mine, I was

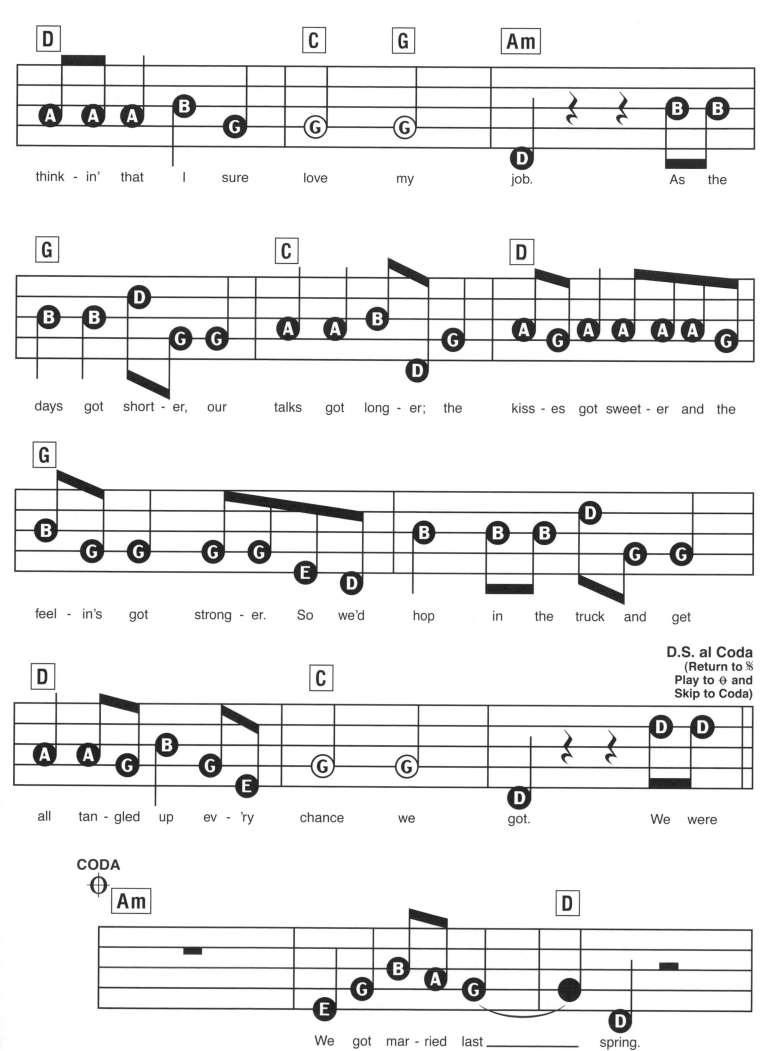

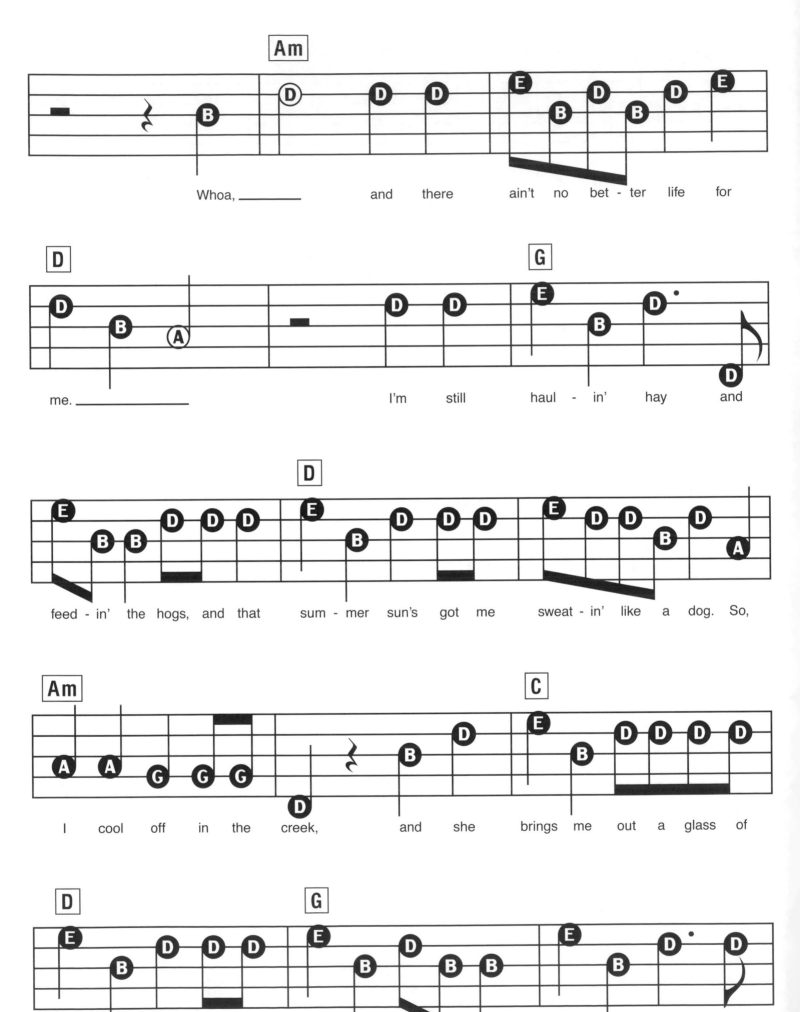

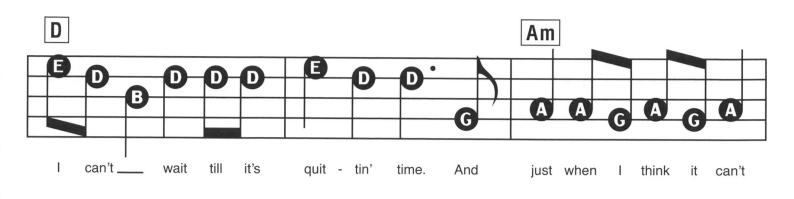

I can't ___ wait till it's quit - tin' time. And just when I think it can't

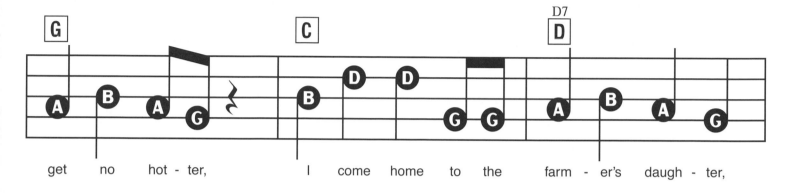

get no hot - ter, I come home to the farm - er's daugh - ter,

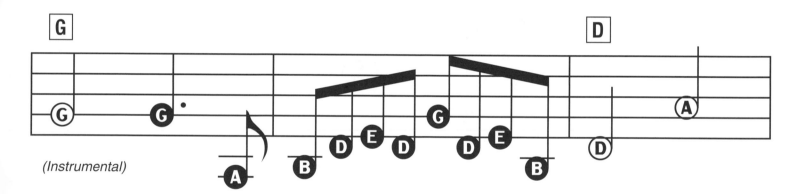

(Instrumental)

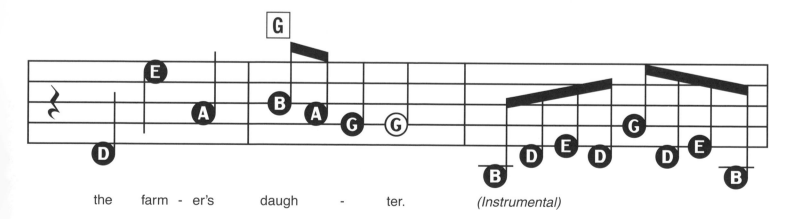

the farm - er's daugh - ter. *(Instrumental)*

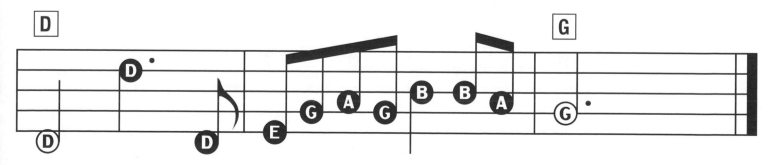

Follow Your Arrow

Registration 4
Rhythm: Country Swing or Fox Trot

Words and Music by Kacey Musgraves,
Shane McAnally and Brandy Clark

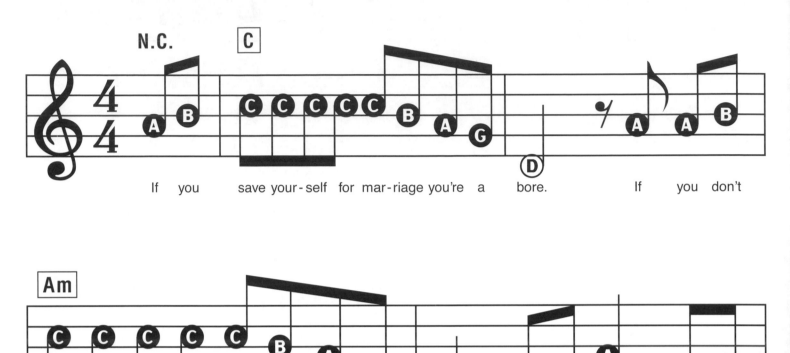

N.C.   C

If you save your-self for mar-riage you're a bore.   If you don't

Am

save your-self for mar-riage, you're a hor - ri - ble per - son.   If

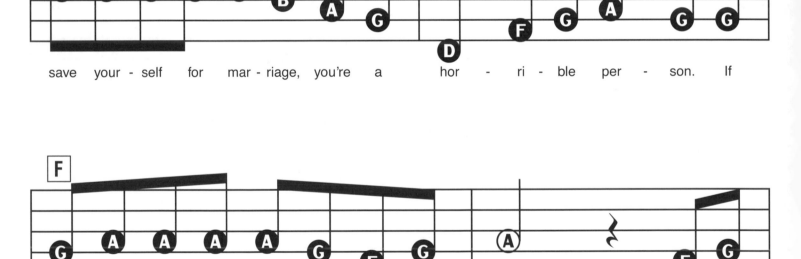

F

you won't have a drink, then you're a prude.   But they'll

Dm   G

call you a drunk as soon as you down the first one.   If

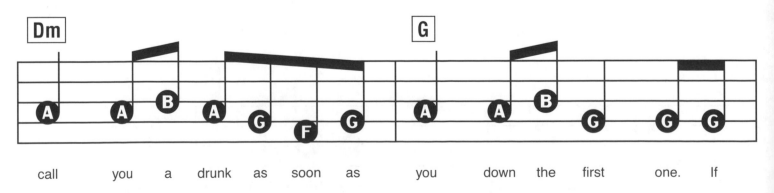

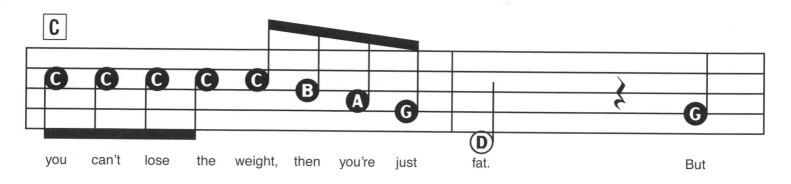

C

you can't lose the weight, then you're just fat. But

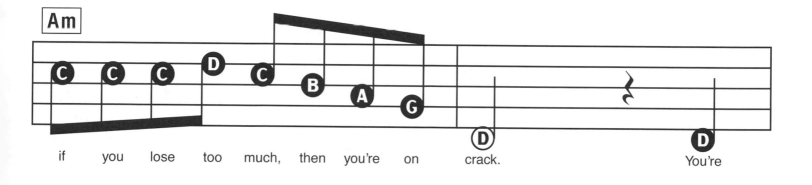

Am

if you lose too much, then you're on crack. You're

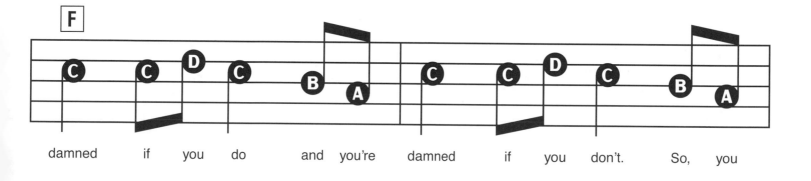

F

damned if you do and you're damned if you don't. So, you

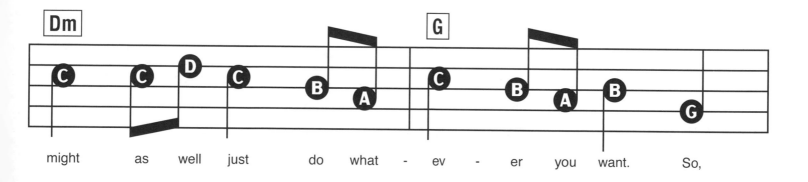

Dm   **G**

might as well just do what - ev - er you want. So,

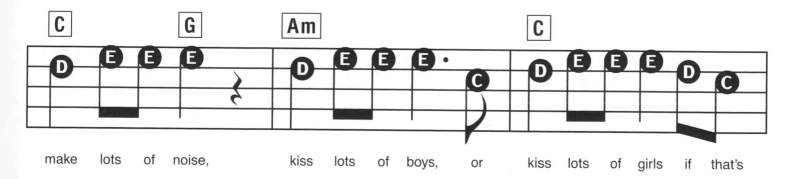

C   **G**   **Am**   **C**

make lots of noise, kiss lots of boys, or kiss lots of girls if that's

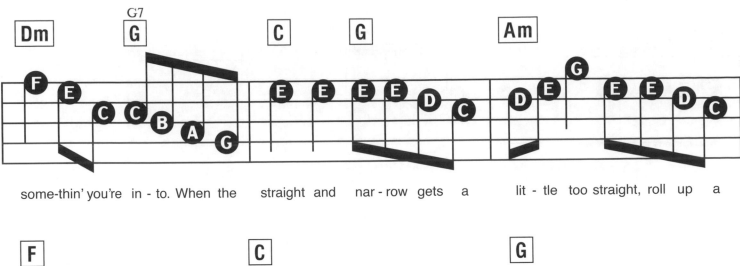

some-thin' you're in - to. When the straight and nar - row gets a lit - tle too straight, roll up a

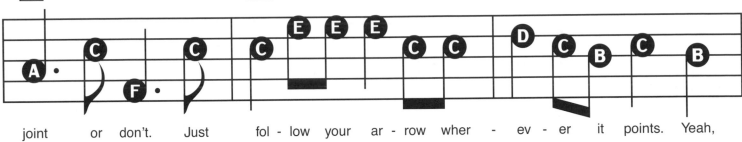

joint or don't. Just fol - low your ar - row wher - ev - er it points. Yeah,

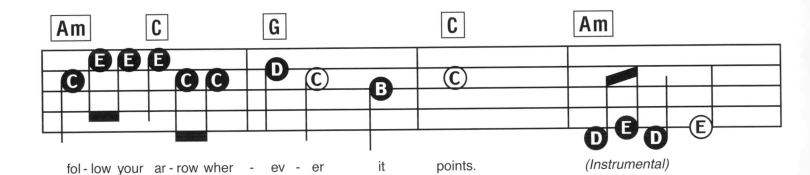

fol - low your ar - row wher - ev - er it points. *(Instrumental)*

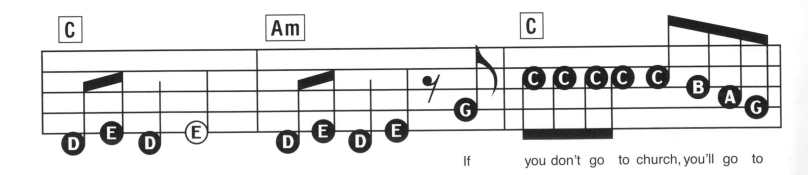

If you don't go to church, you'll go to

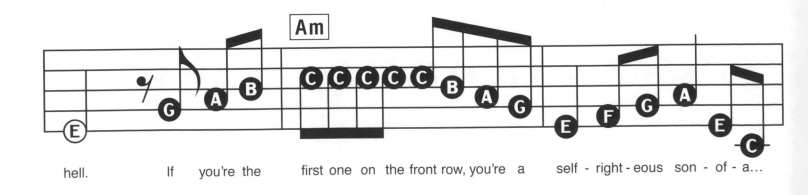

hell. If you're the first one on the front row, you're a self - right - eous son - of - a...

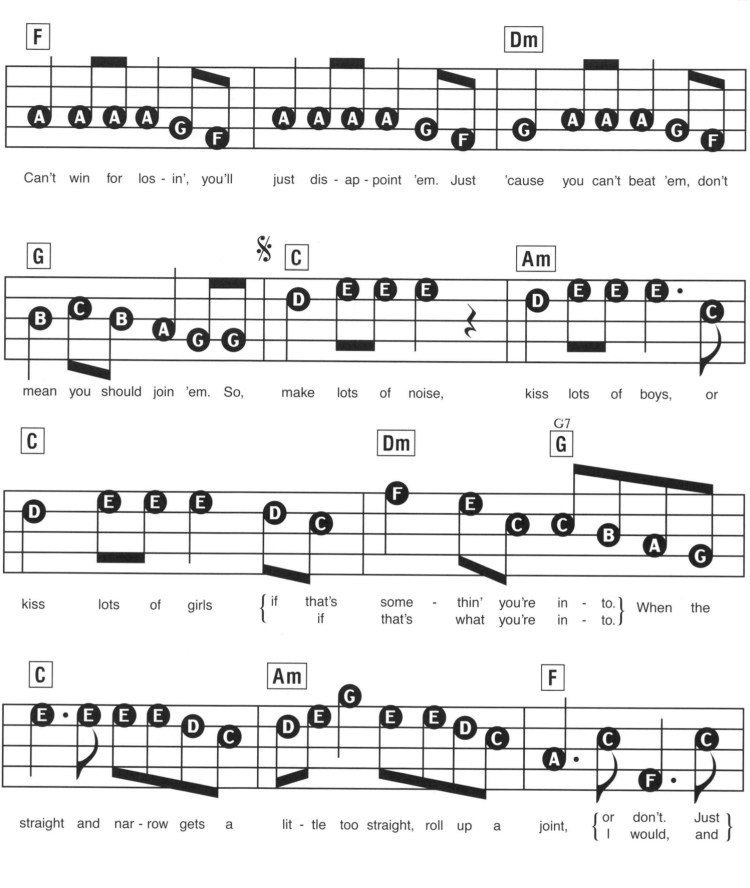

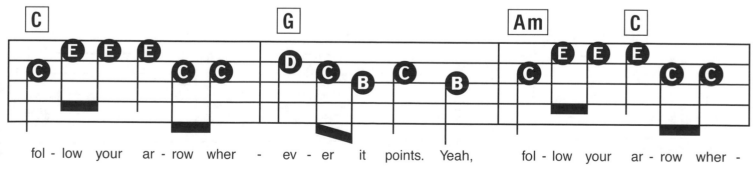

The House That Built Me

Registration 1
Rhythm: Folk or 4/4 Ballad

Words and Music by Tom Douglas
and Allen Shamblin

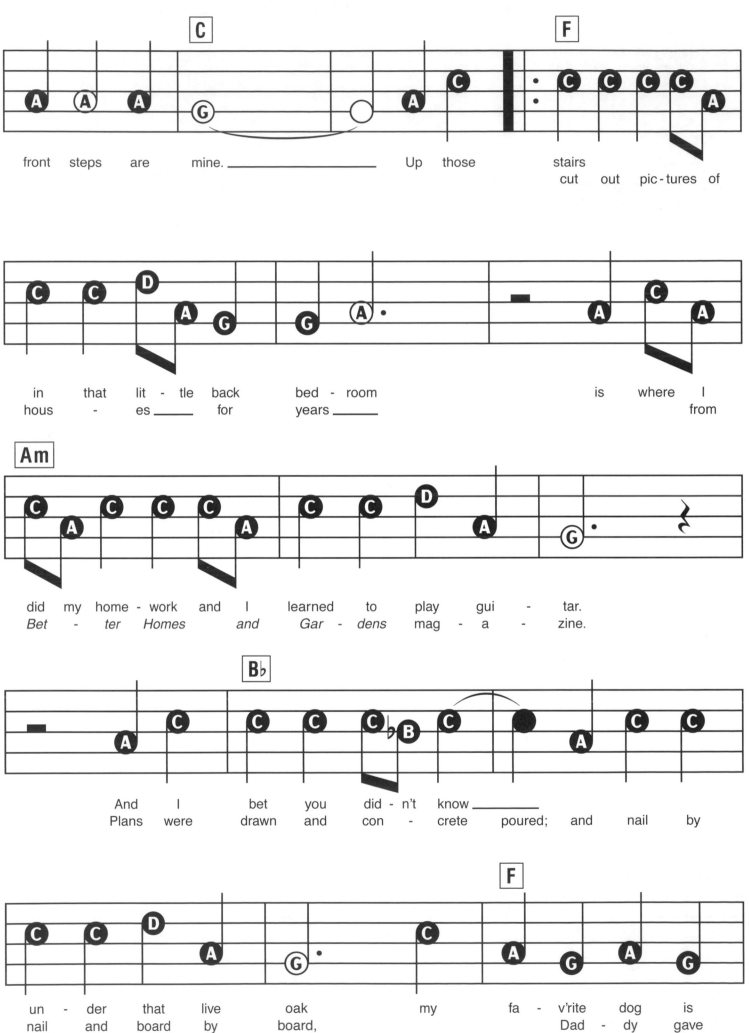

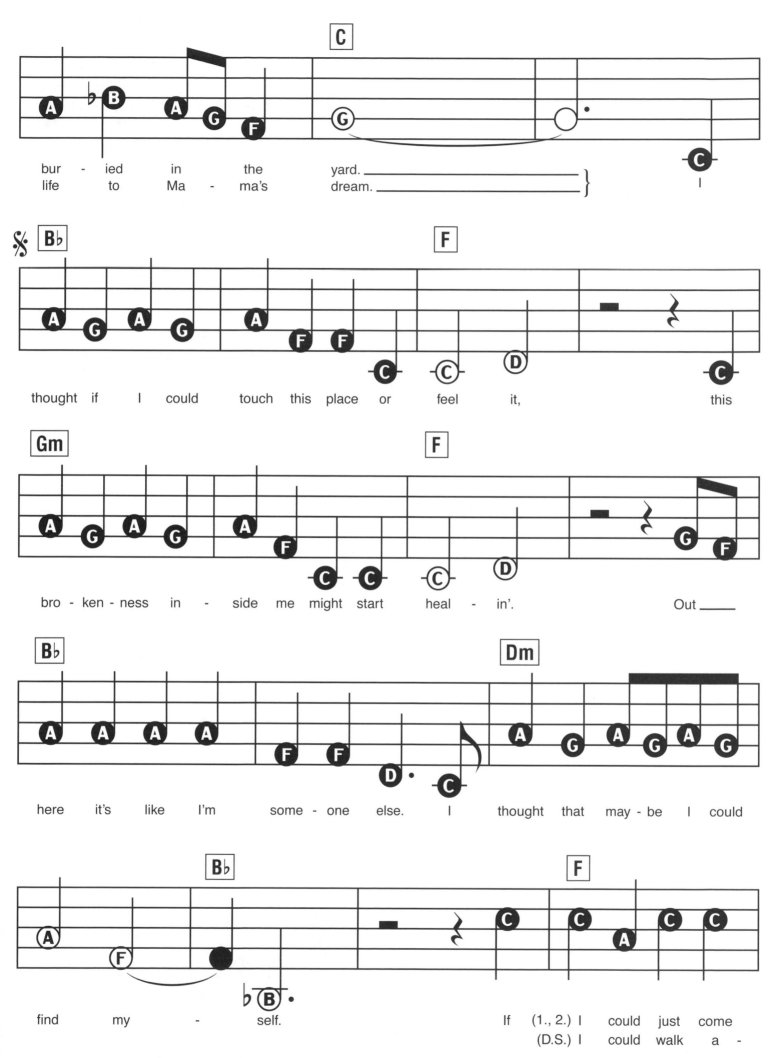

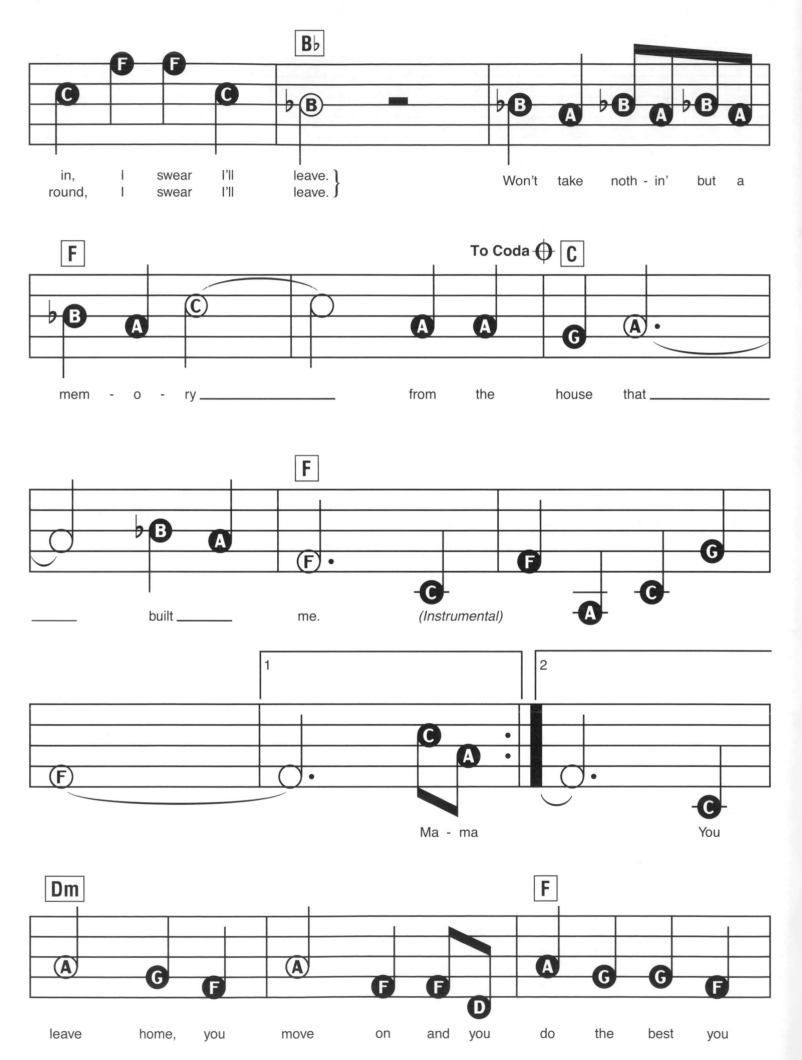

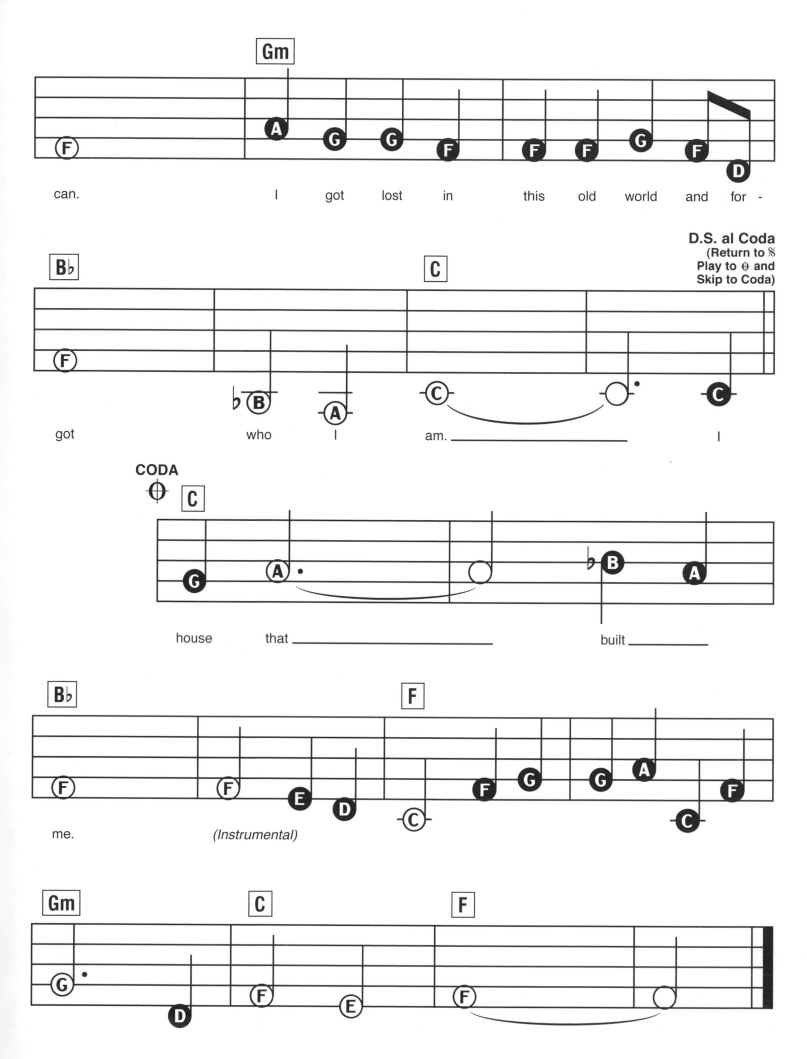

Gm

F

can.   I got lost in this old world and for -

D.S. al Coda
(Return to 𝄋
Play to ⊕ and
Skip to Coda)

B♭   C

F

got   who I am. _____   I

CODA
⊕   C

house that _____ built _____

B♭   F

me.   (Instrumental)

Gm   C   F

God Gave Me You

Registration 4
Rhythm: Country Pop or 8-Beat

Words and Music by
Dave Barnes

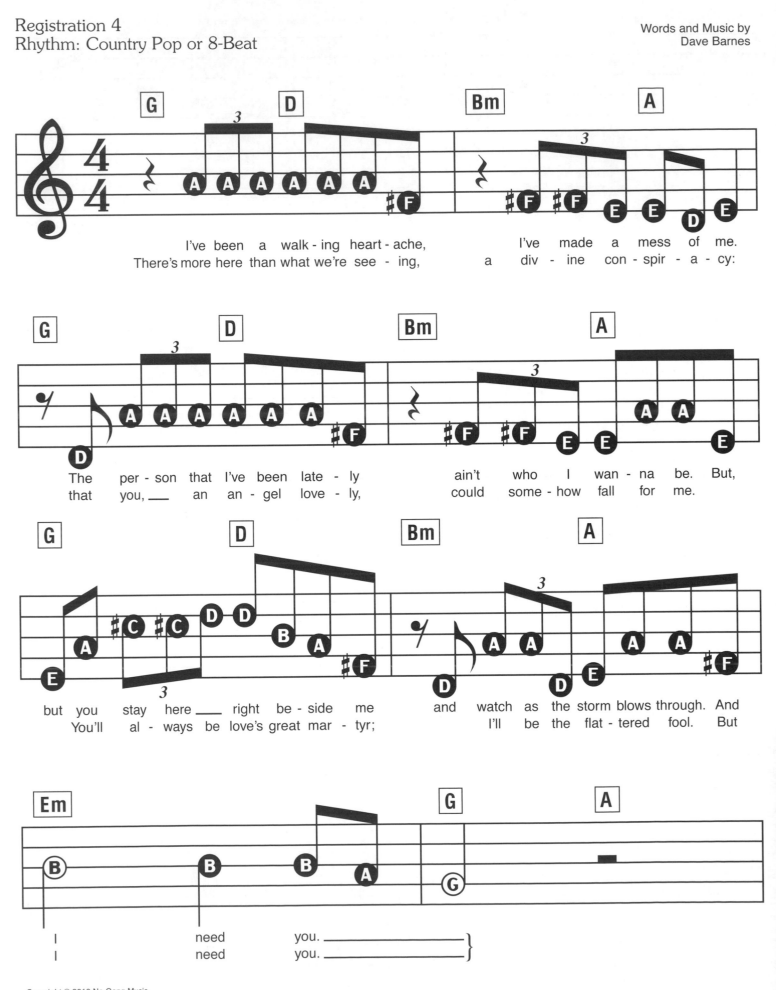

47

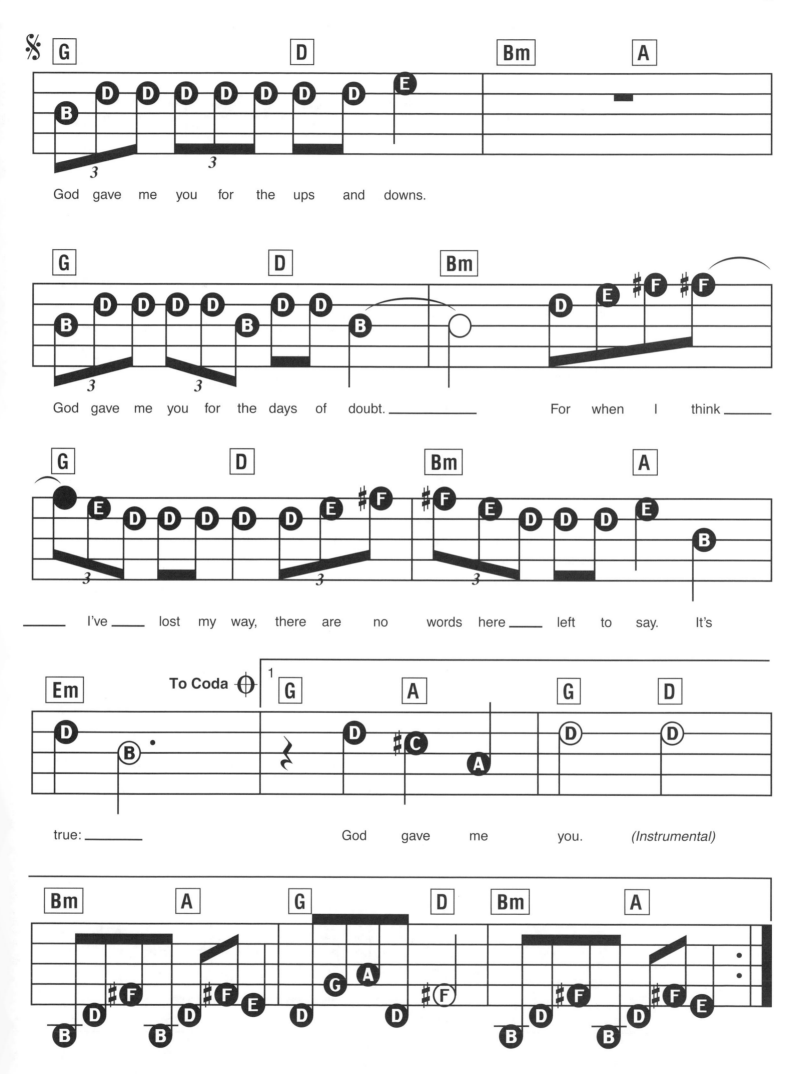

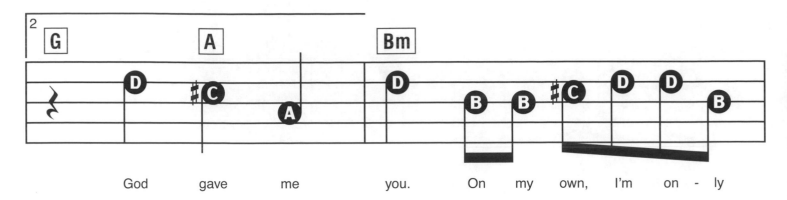

God gave me you. On my own, I'm on - ly

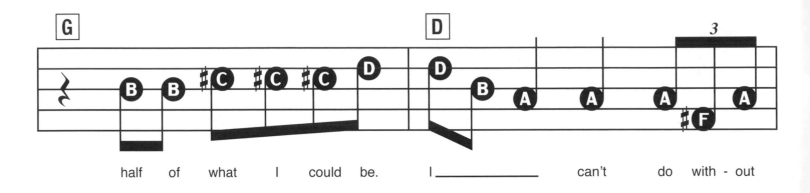

half of what I could be. I _____ can't do with - out

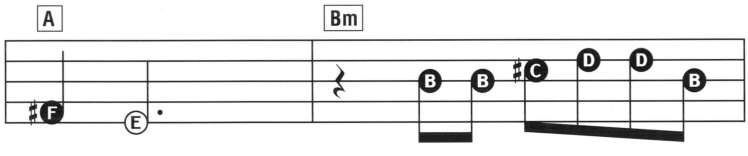

you. _____ We are stitched to - geth - er;

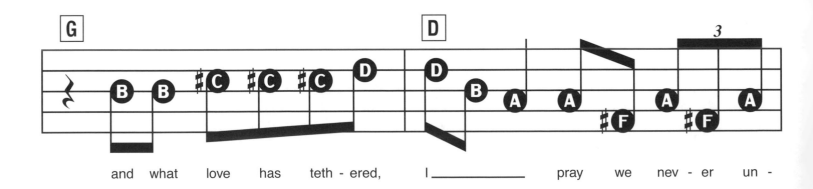

and what love has teth - ered, I _____ pray we nev - er un -

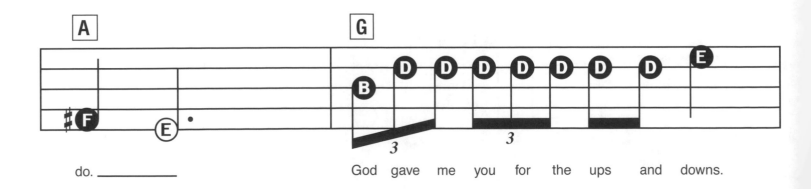

do. _____ God gave me you for the ups and downs.

D.S. al Coda
(Return to %
Play to ⊕ and
Skip to Coda)

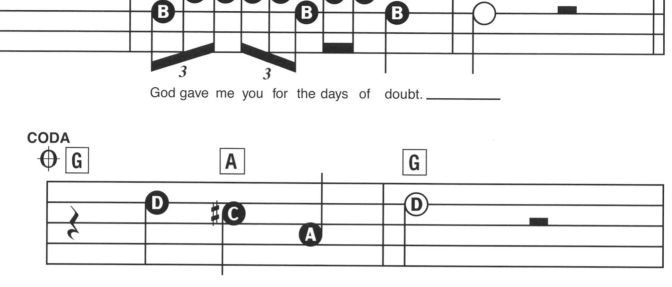

God gave me you for the days of doubt. _____

CODA

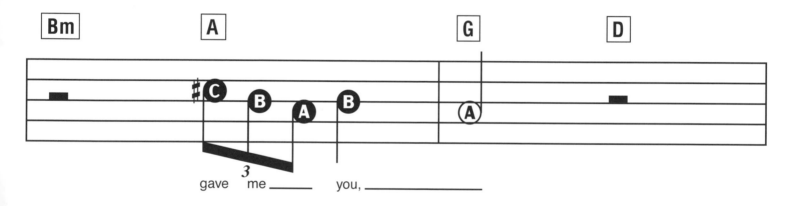

God gave me you,

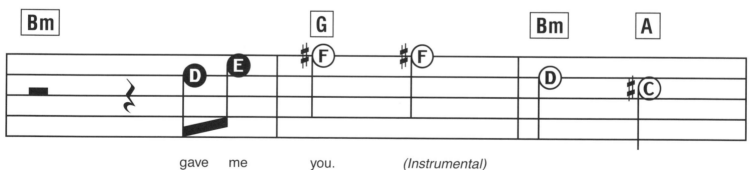

gave me ____ you, _____

gave me you. *(Instrumental)*

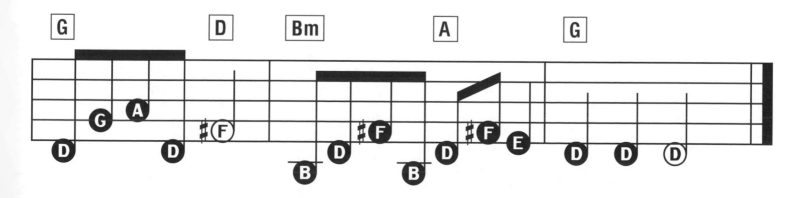

I Hope You Dance

Registration 8
Rhythm: Country Pop or Ballad

Words and Music by Tia Sillers
and Mark D. Sanders

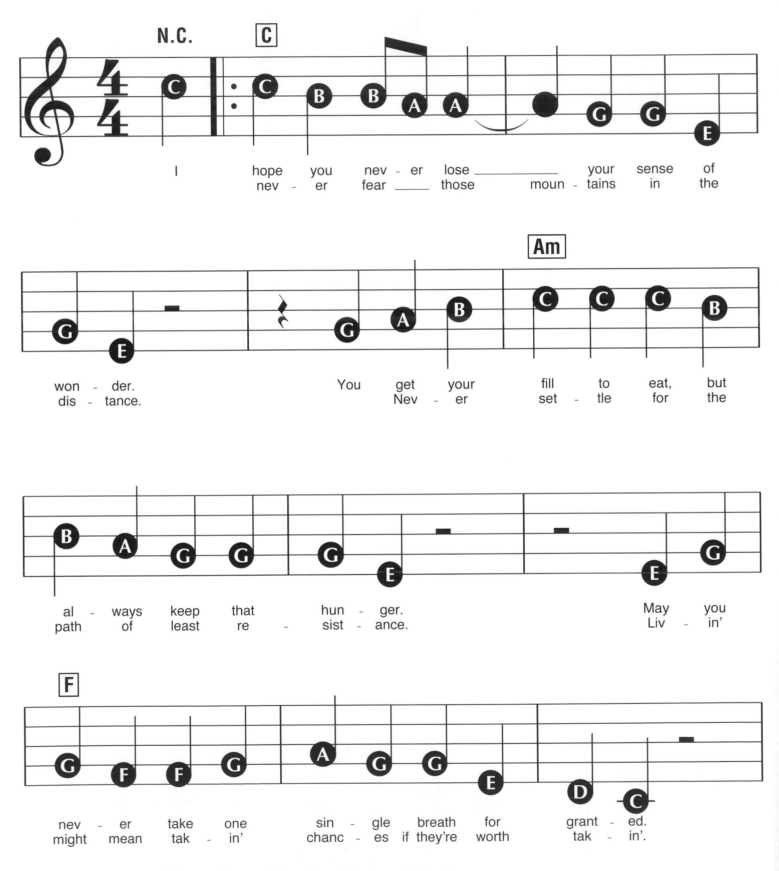

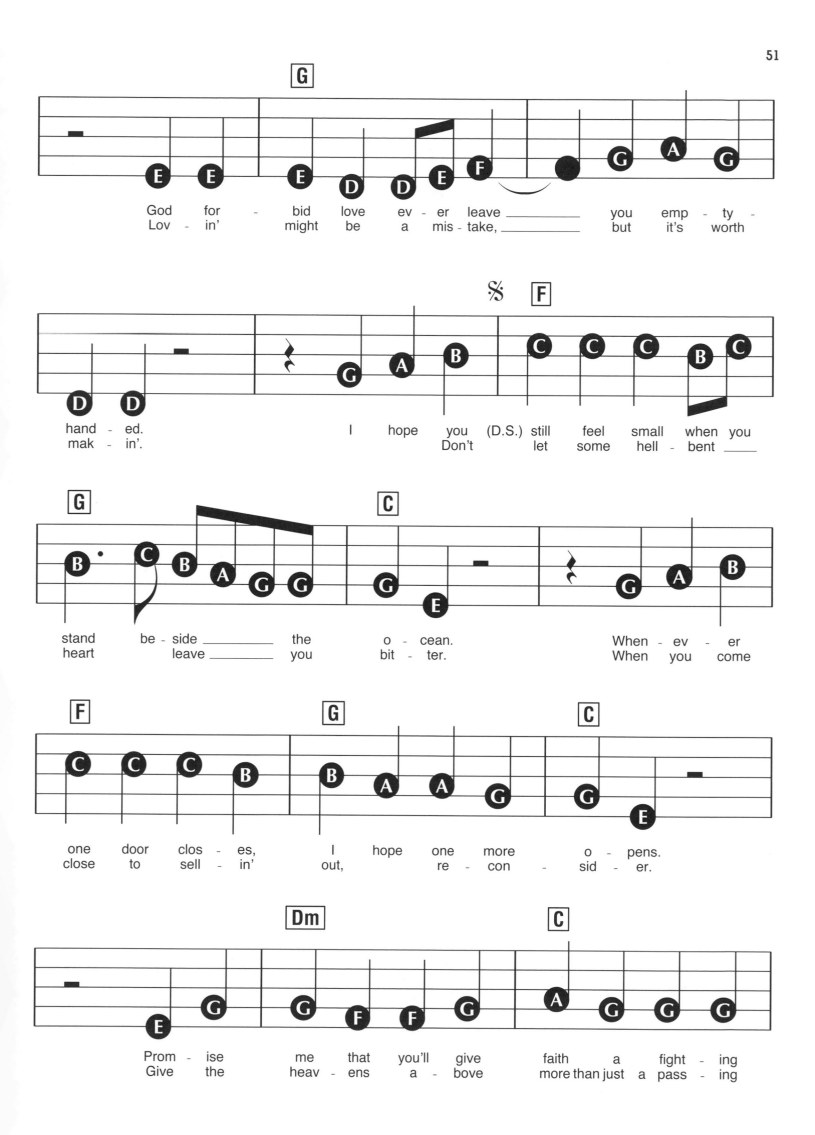

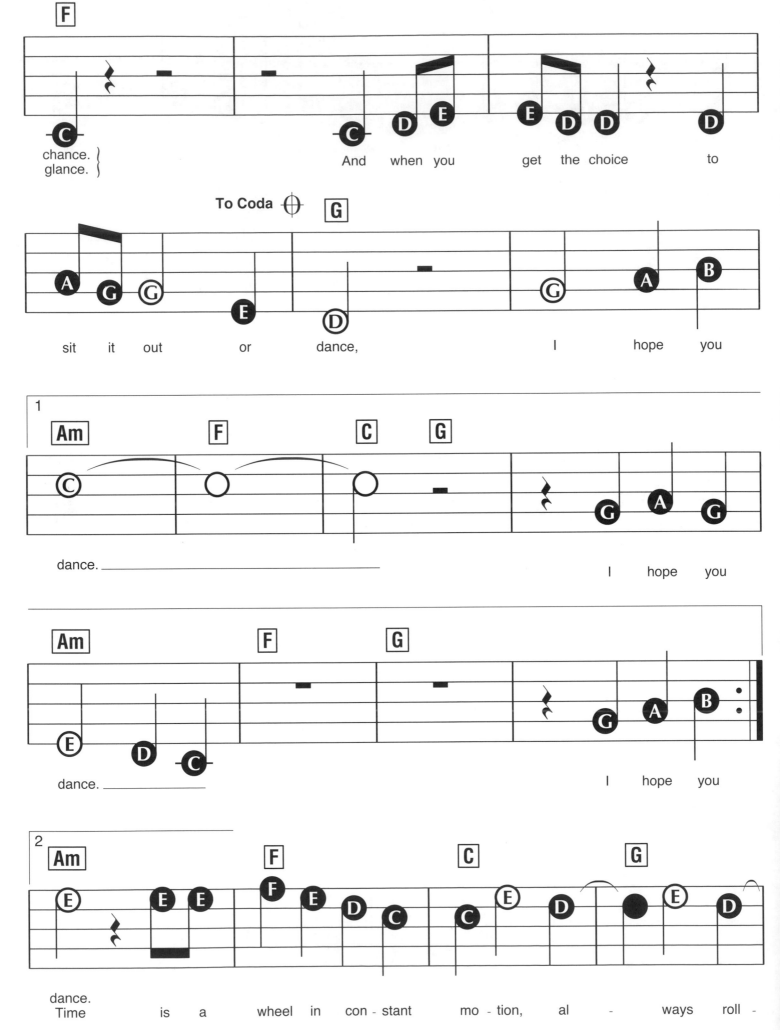

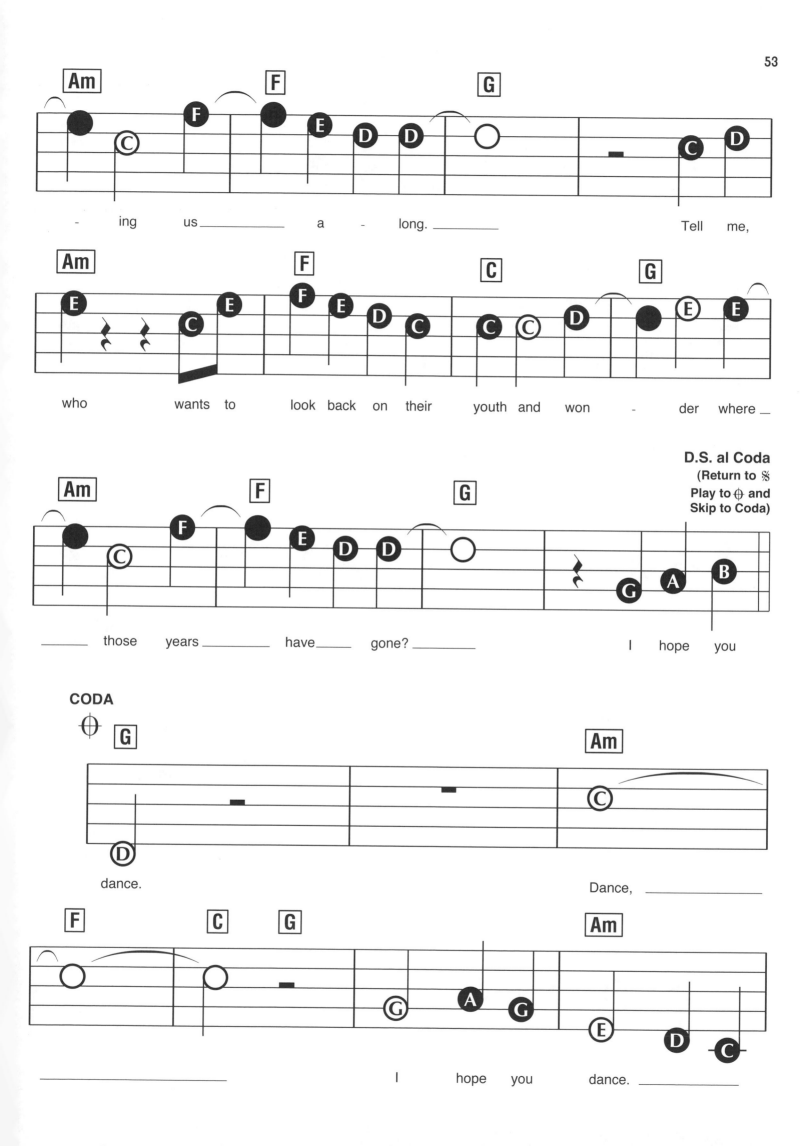

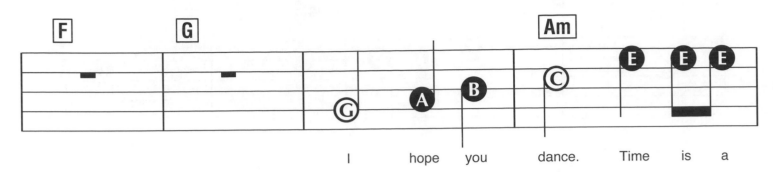

I hope you dance. Time is a

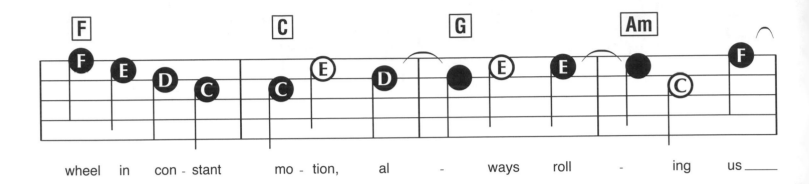

wheel in con - stant mo - tion, al - ways roll - ing us _____

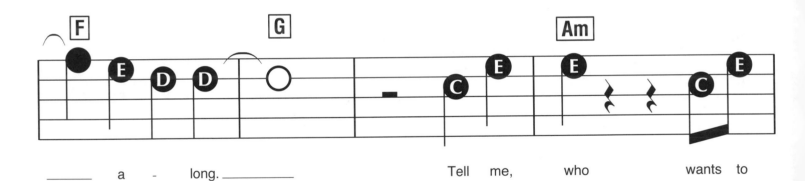

_____ a - long. _____ Tell me, who wants to

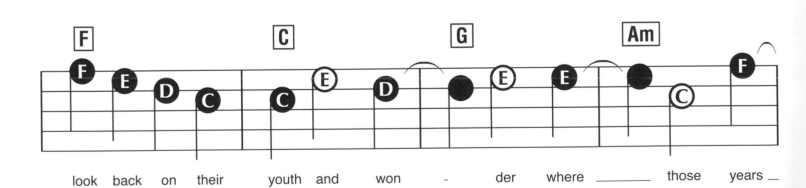

look back on their youth and won - der where _____ those years

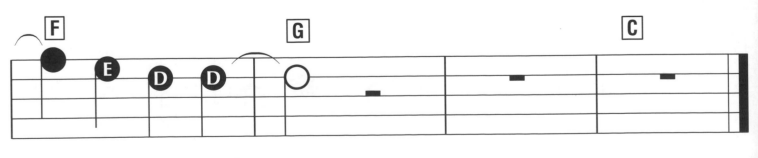

_____ have _____ gone? _____

I Knew You Were Trouble.

Registration 4
Rhythm: Country Pop or Rock

Words and Music by Taylor Swift,
Shellback and Max Martin

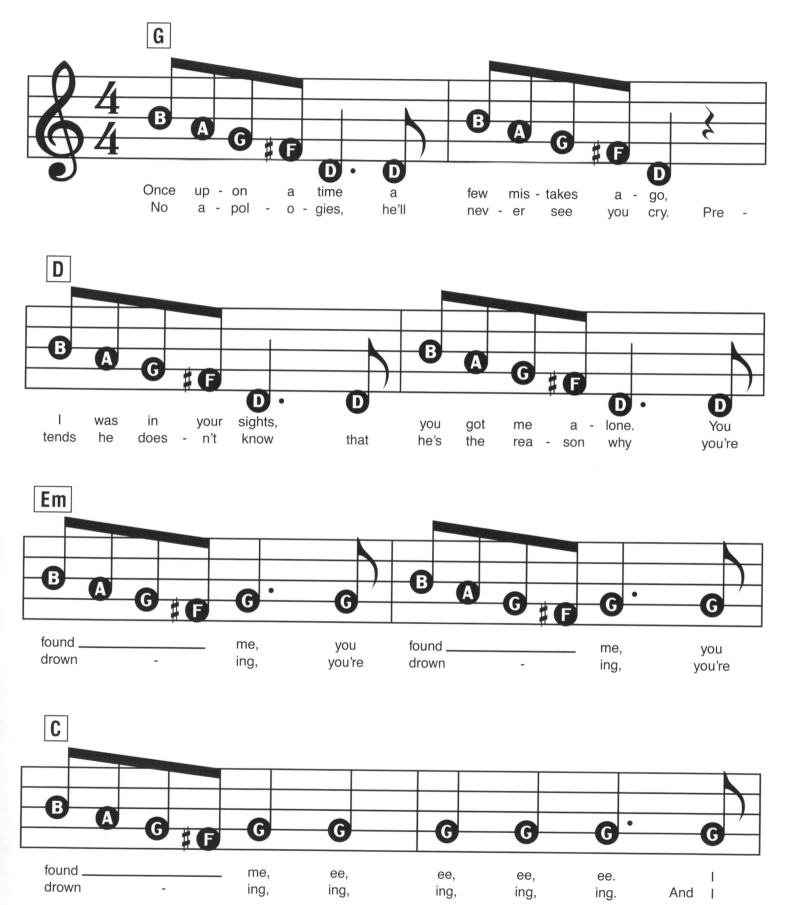

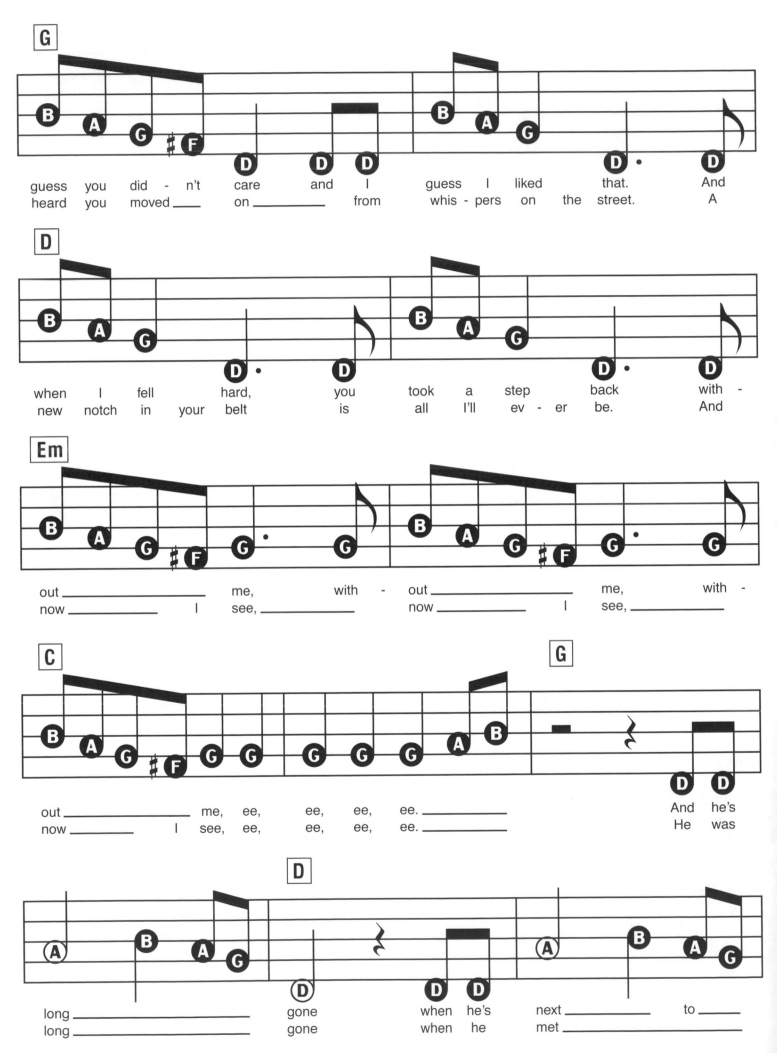

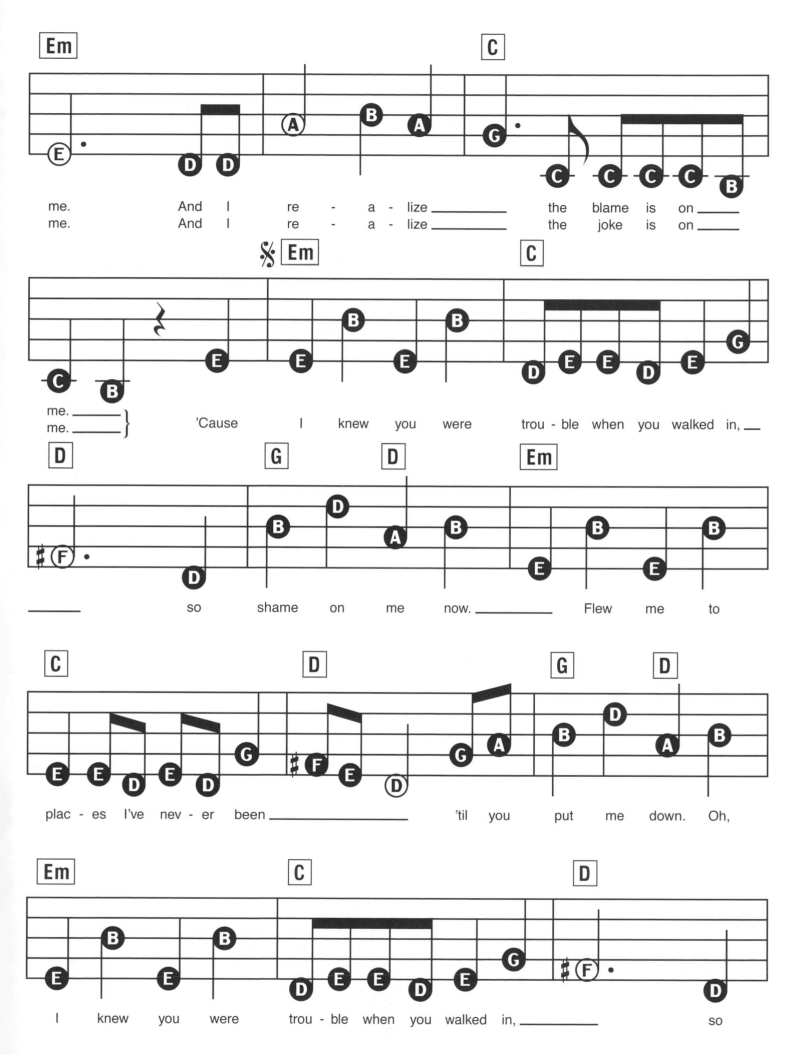

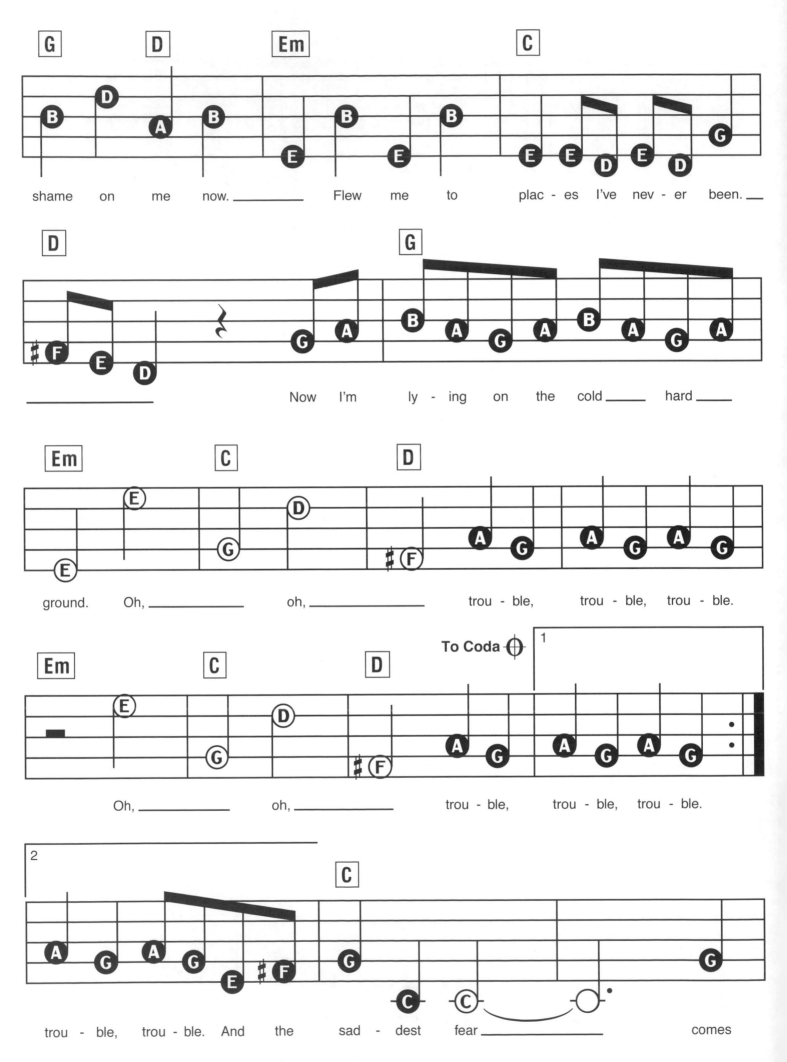

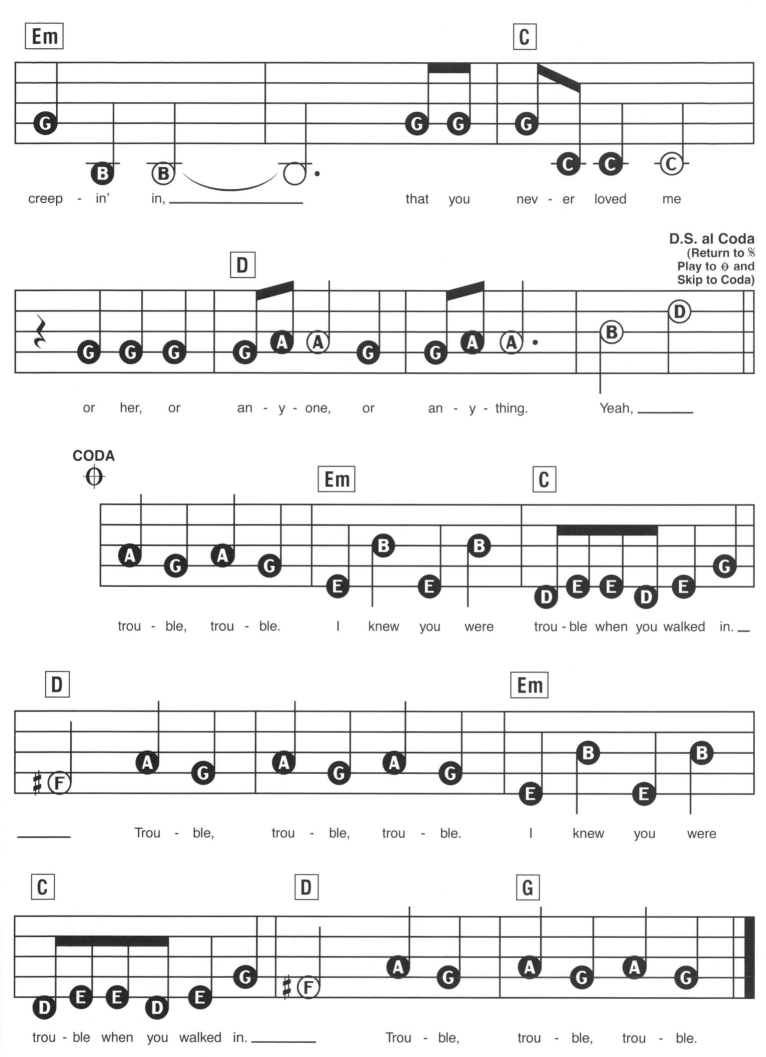

If I Die Young

Registration 4
Rhythm: 8-Beat or Country Pop

Words and Music by
Kimberly Perry

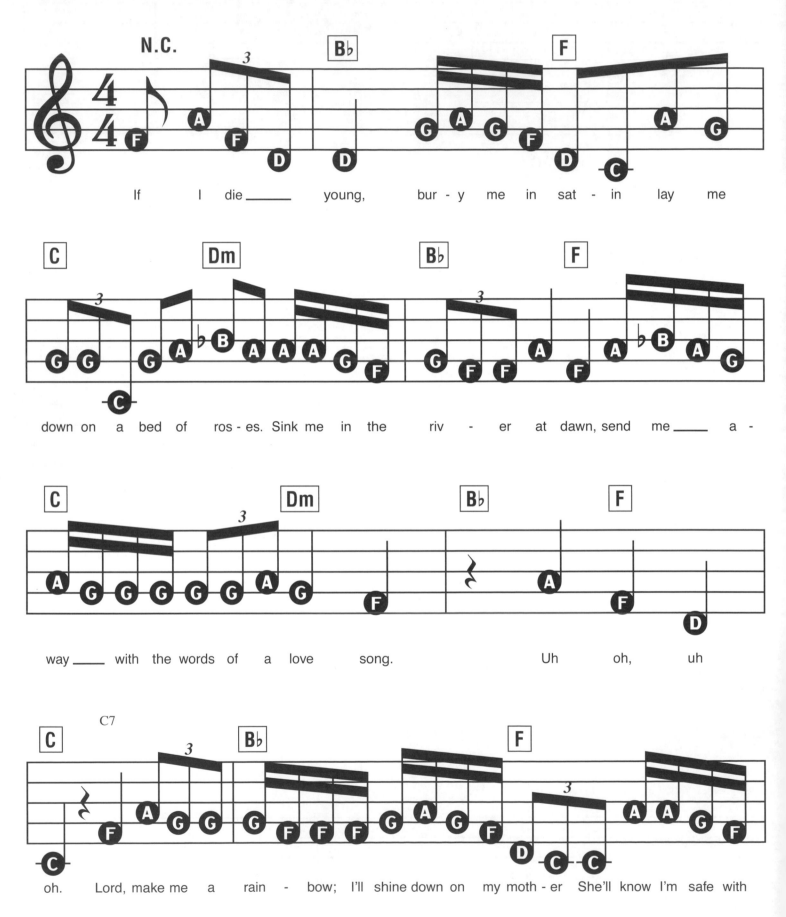

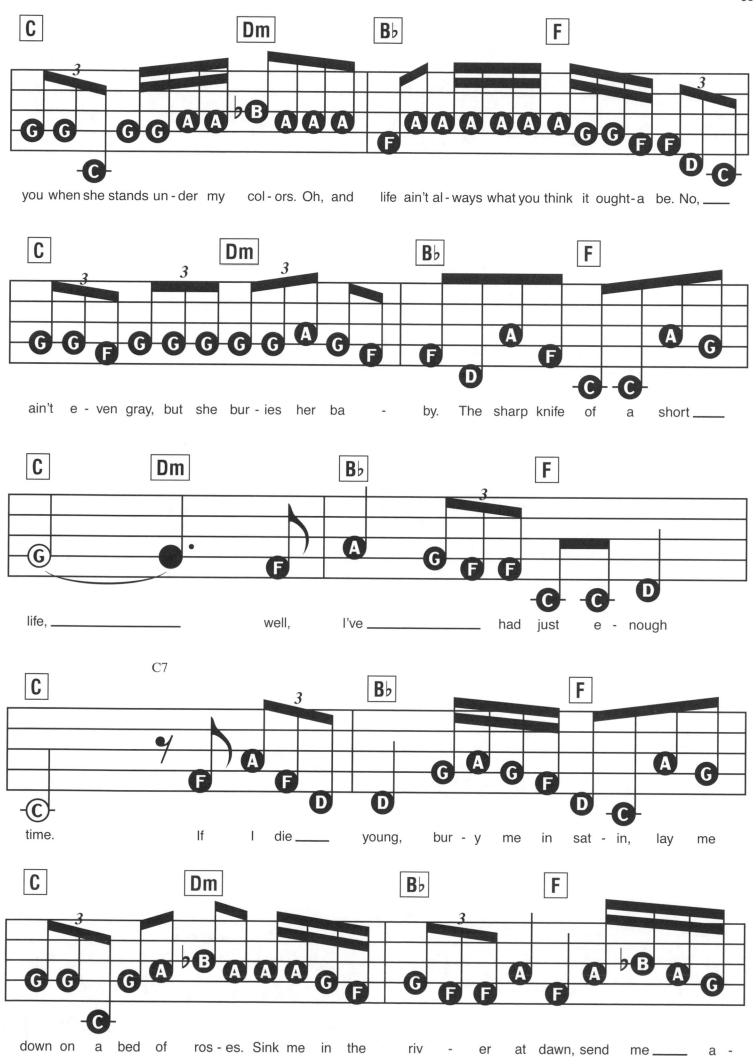

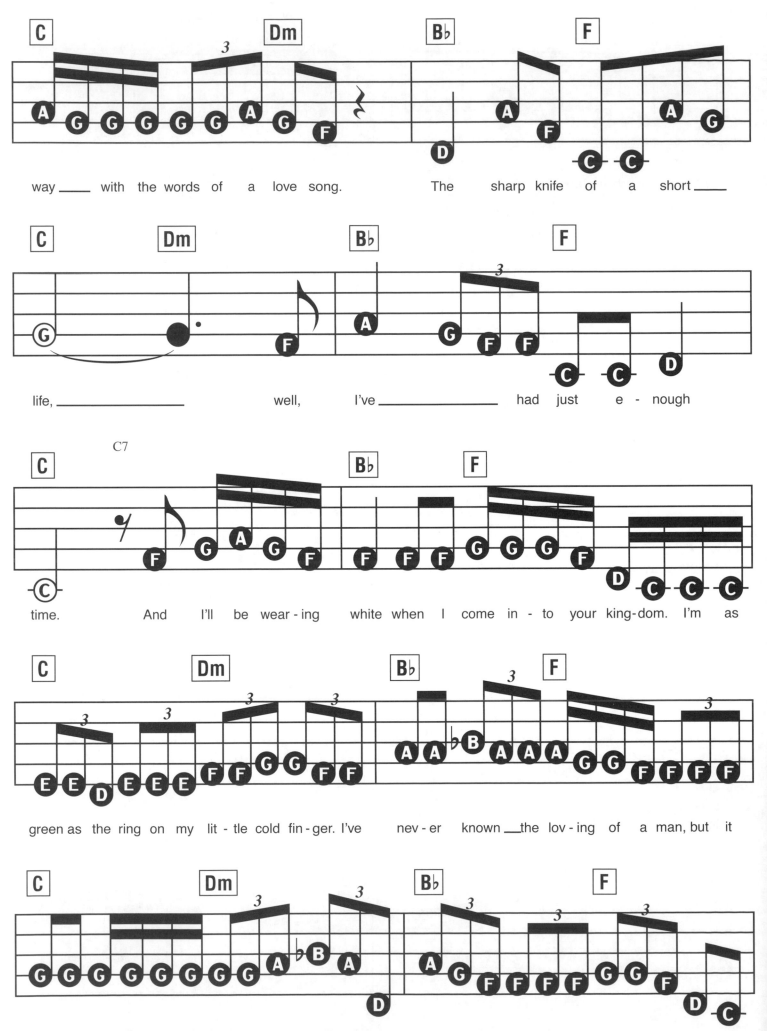

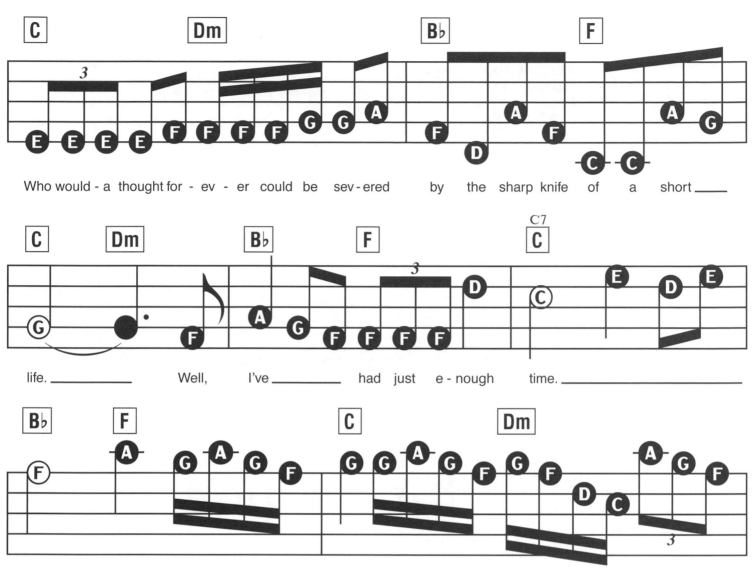

Who would - a thought for - ev - er could be sev - ered by the sharp knife of a short ____

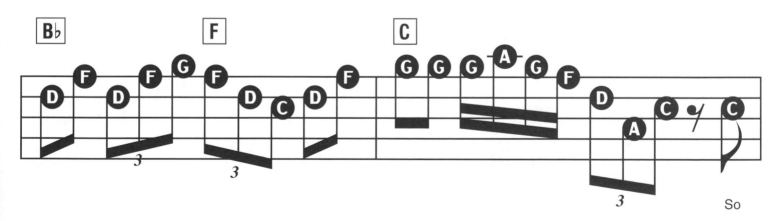

life. _____ Well, I've _____ had just e - nough time. _____

_____ (Instrumental)

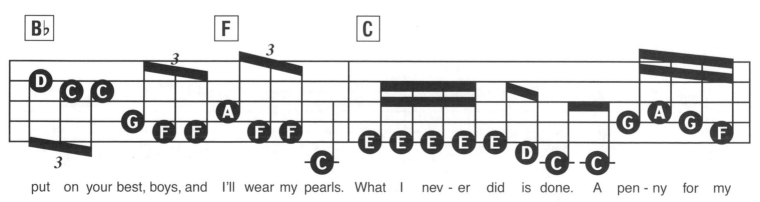

So

put on your best, boys, and I'll wear my pearls. What I nev - er did is done. A pen - ny for my

64

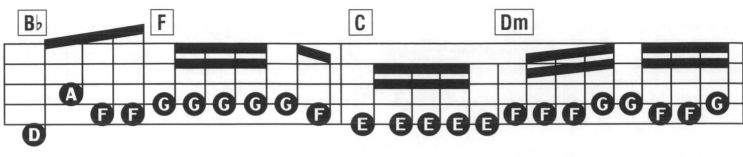

thoughts: oh no, I'll sell 'em for a dol - lar. They're worth so much more af - ter I'm a gon - er. And ___

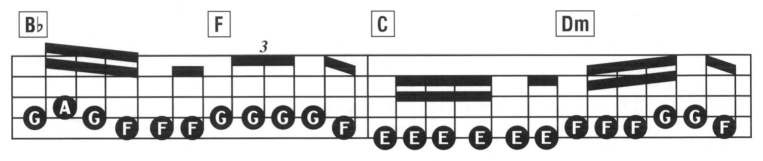

may - be then you'll hear the words I've been sing-ing. Fun - ny, when you're dead how peo - ple start a - lis - t'nin'.

C7

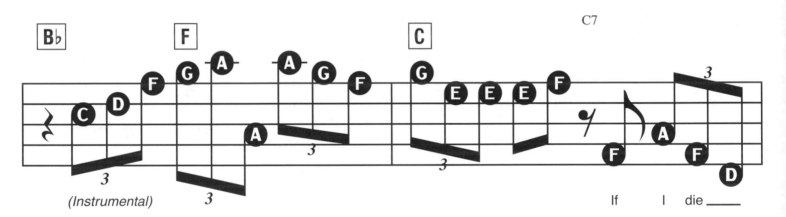

(Instrumental)   If   I   die ___

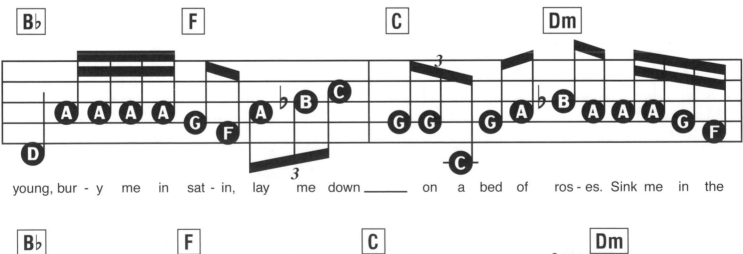

young, bur - y me in sat - in, lay   me down ___ on a bed of ros - es. Sink me in the

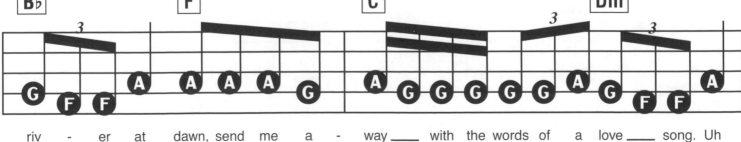

riv - er at dawn, send me a - way ___ with the words of a love ___ song. Uh

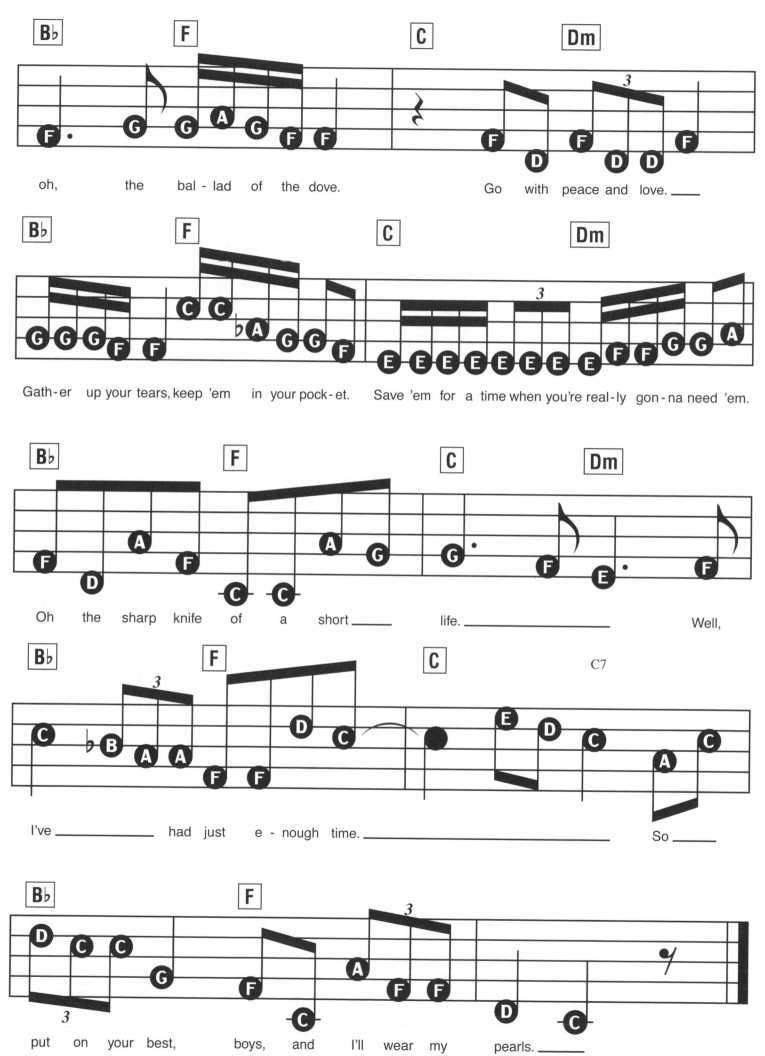

Little Bit of Everything

Registration 4
Rhythm: Country Rock or 8-Beat

Words and Music by Brad Warren,
Brett Warren and Kevin Rudolph

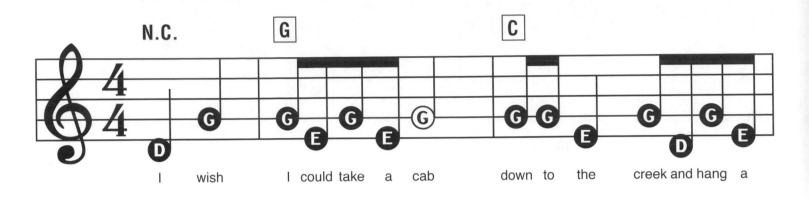

I wish I could take a cab down to the creek and hang a

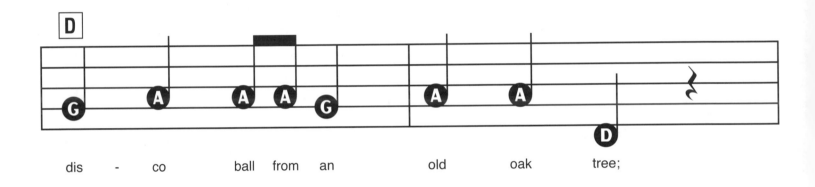

dis - co ball from an old oak tree;

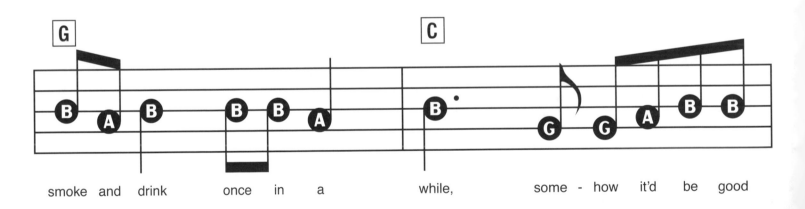

smoke and drink once in a while, some - how it'd be good

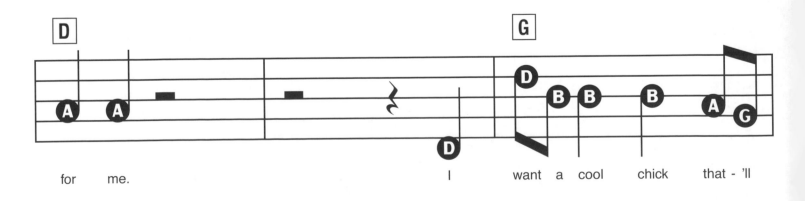

for me. I want a cool chick that - 'll

67

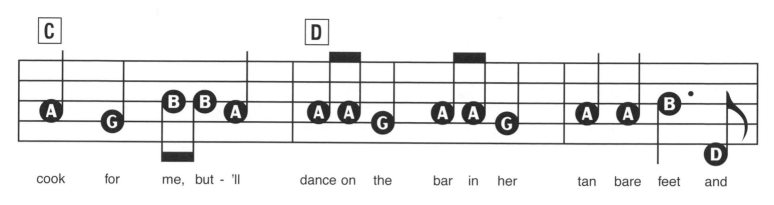

cook for me, but - 'll dance on the bar in her tan bare feet and

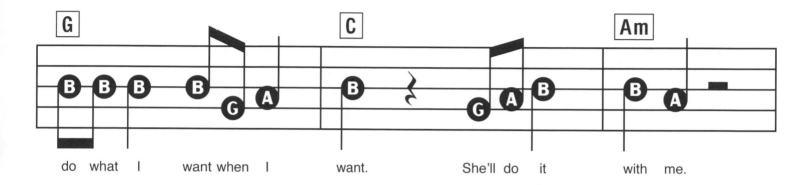

do what I want when I want. She'll do it with me.

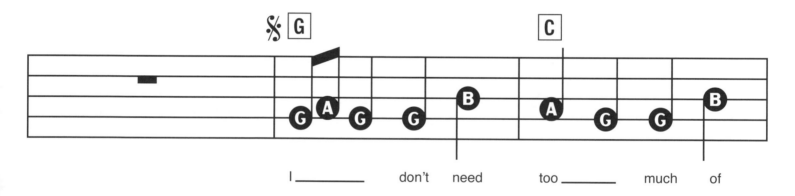

I _____ don't need too _____ much of

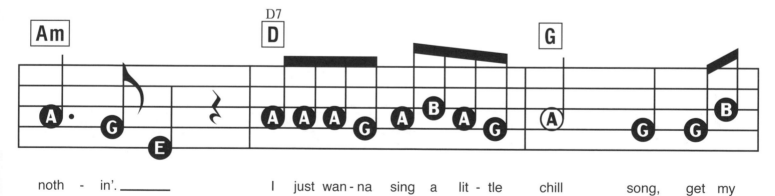

noth - in'. _____ I just wan-na sing a lit-tle chill song, get my

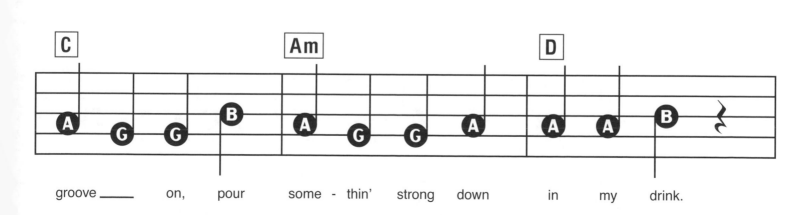

groove _____ on, pour some-thin' strong down in my drink.

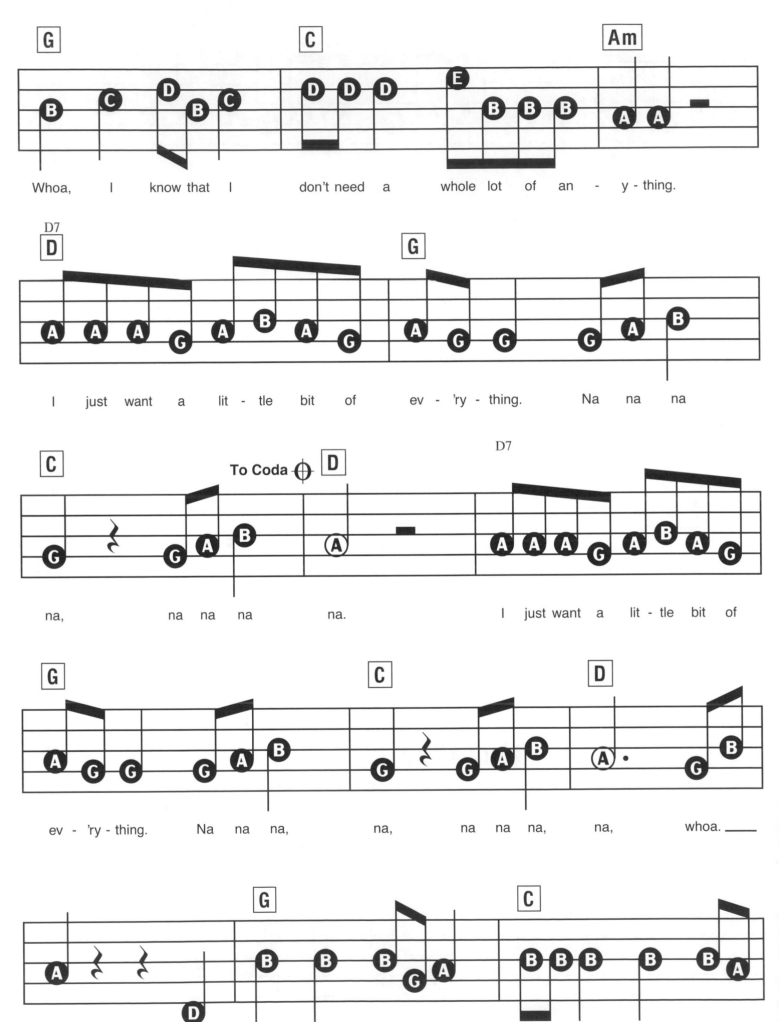

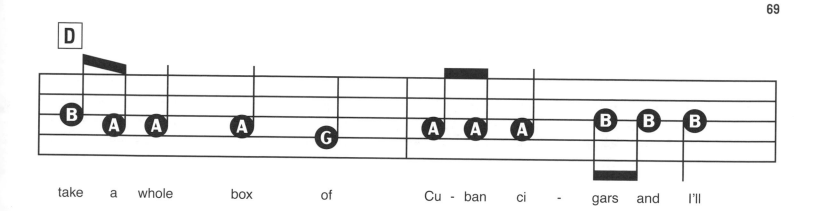

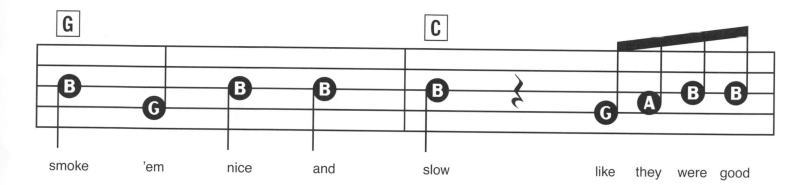

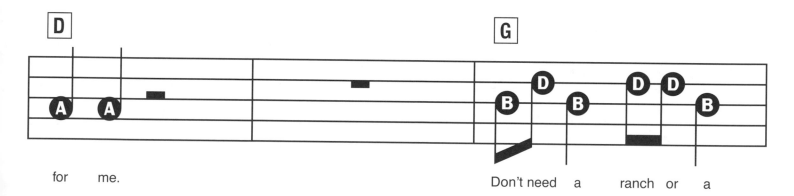

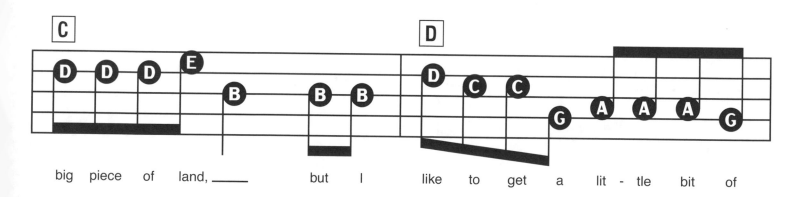

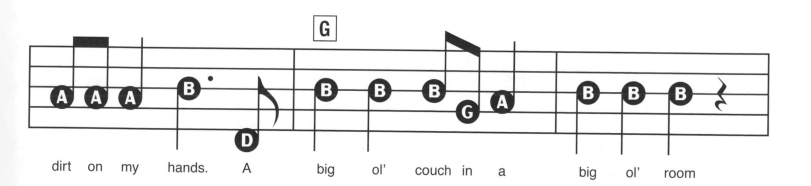

D.S. al Coda
(Return to %
Play to ⊕ and
Skip to Coda)

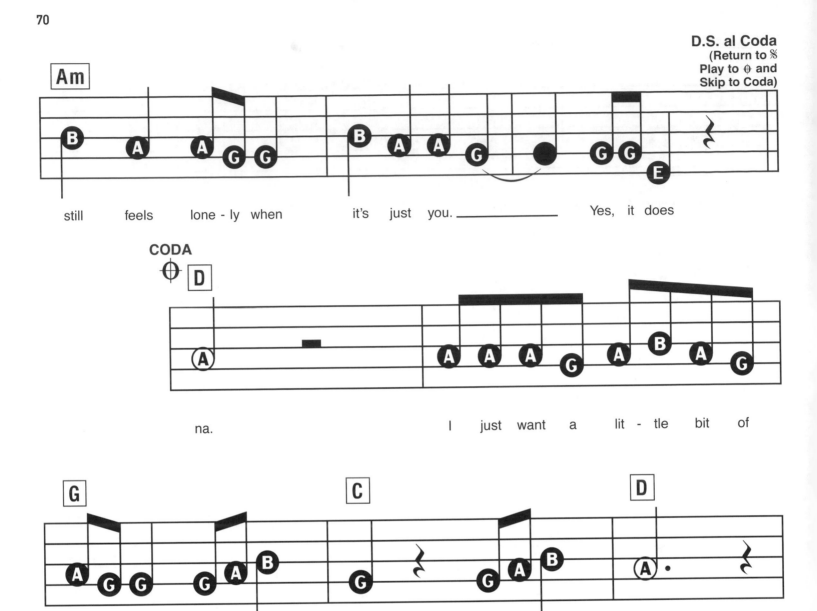

still   feels   lone - ly   when   it's   just   you. _____   Yes, it does

CODA

na.   I   just   want   a   lit - tle   bit   of

ev - 'ry - thing.   Na   na   na   na,   na   na   na   na.

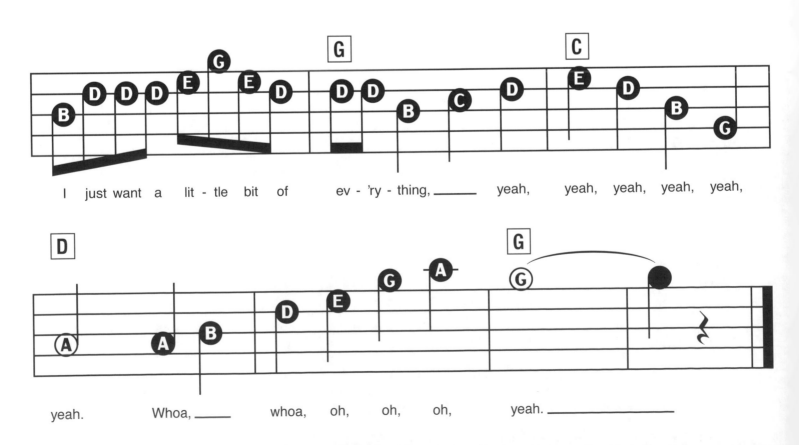

I   just want   a   lit - tle   bit   of   ev - 'ry - thing, _____ yeah,   yeah,   yeah,   yeah,   yeah,

yeah.   Whoa, _____   whoa,   oh,   oh,   oh,   yeah. _____

Need You Now

Registration 4
Rhythm: 8-Beat or Rock

Words and Music by Hillary Scott,
Charles Kelley, Dave Haywood
and Josh Kear

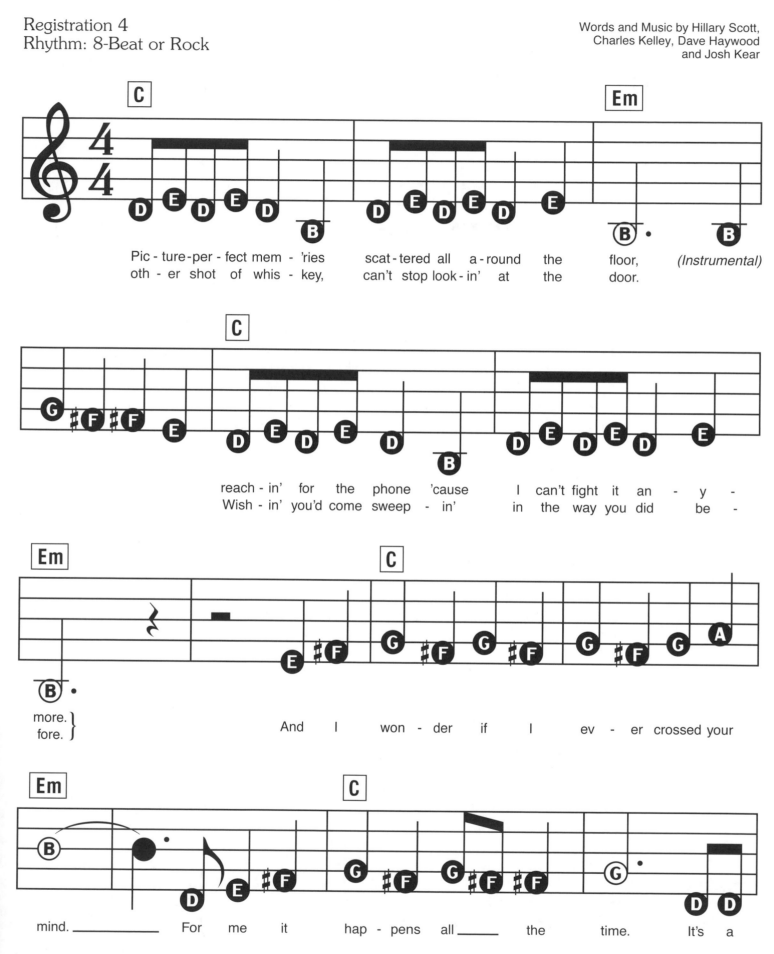

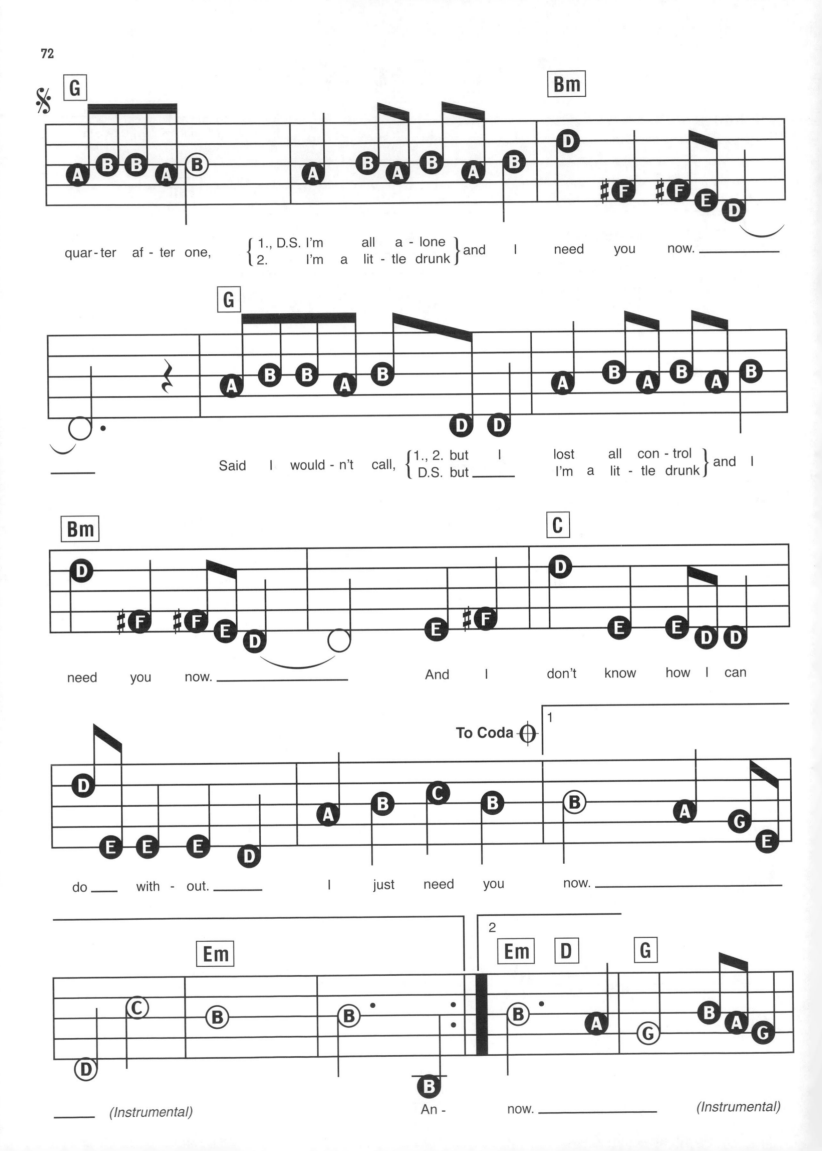

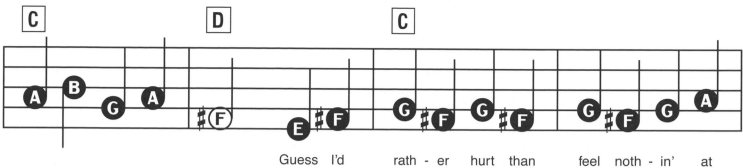

Guess I'd rath - er hurt than feel noth - in' at

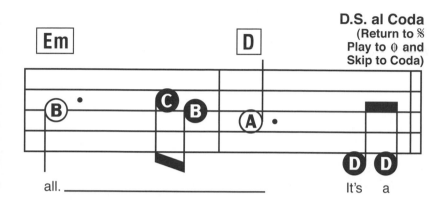
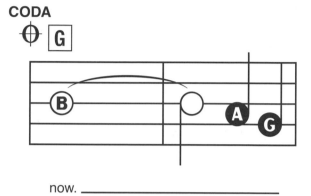

all. _____ It's a now. _____

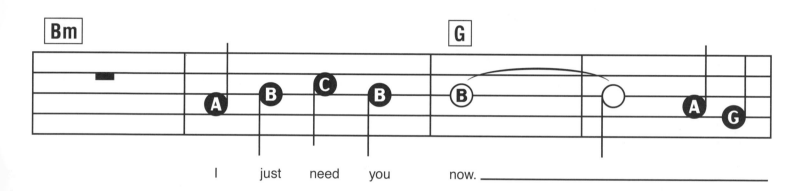

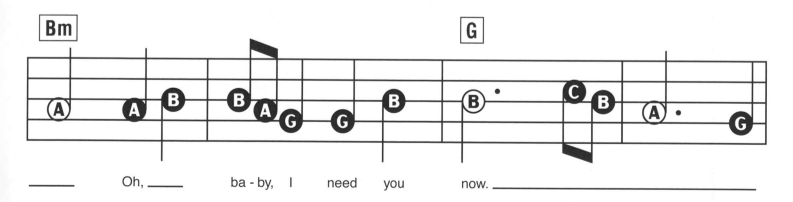

I just need you now. _____

Oh, _____ ba - by, I need you now. _____

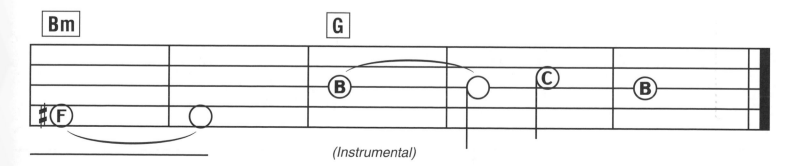

(Instrumental)

She's Everything

Registration 4
Rhythm: 8-Beat or Country Rock

Words and Music by Brad Paisley
and Wil Nance

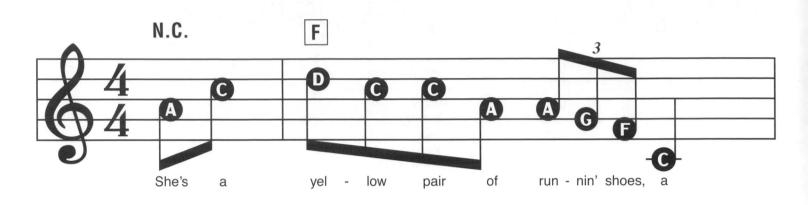

She's a yel - low pair of run - nin' shoes, a

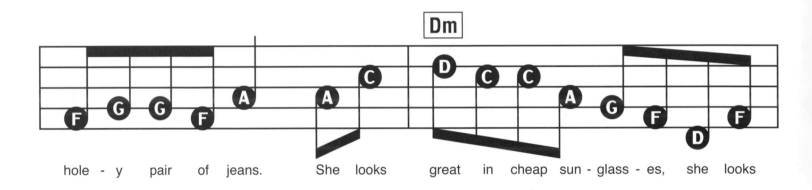

hole - y pair of jeans. She looks great in cheap sun - glass - es, she looks

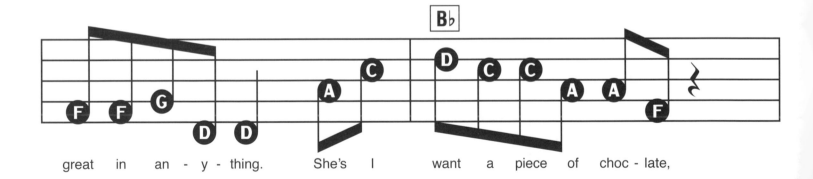

great in an - y - thing. She's I want a piece of choc - late,

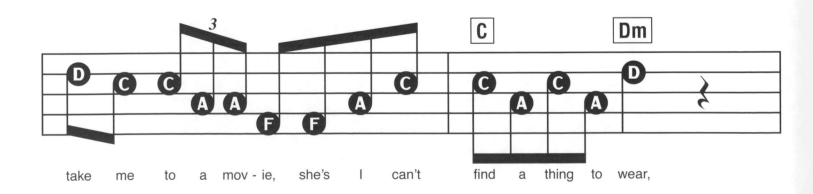

take me to a mov - ie, she's I can't find a thing to wear,

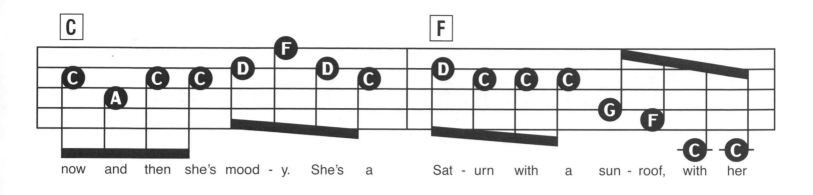

now and then she's mood - y. She's a Sat - urn with a sun - roof, with her

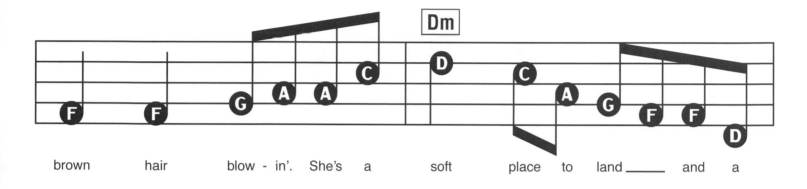

brown hair blow - in'. She's a soft place to land _____ and a

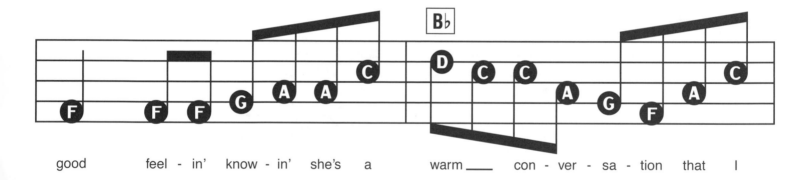

good feel - in' know - in' she's a warm _____ con - ver - sa - tion that I

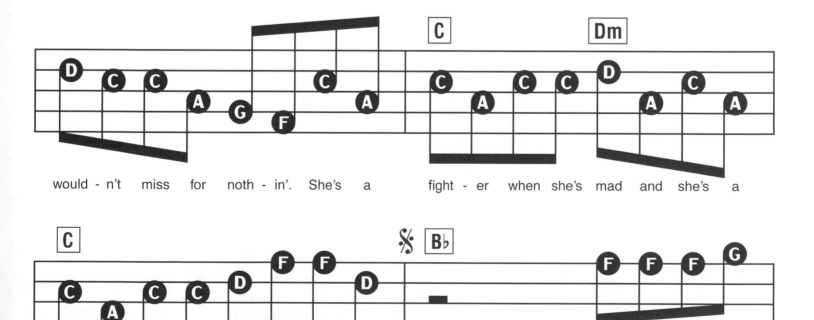

would - n't miss for noth - in'. She's a fight - er when she's mad and she's a

lov - er when she's lov - in'. And she's ev - 'ry - thing I

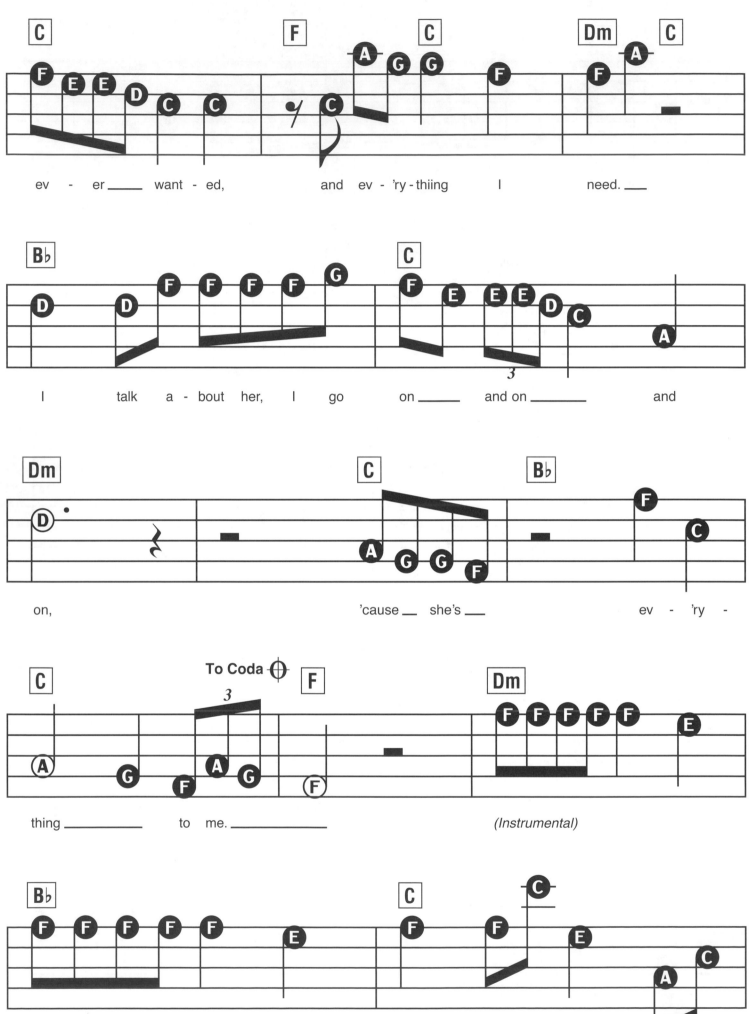

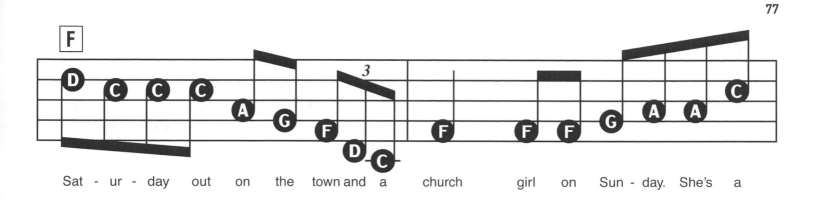

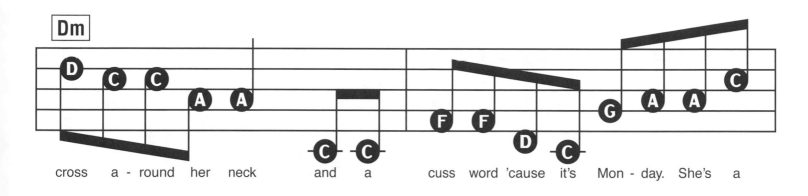

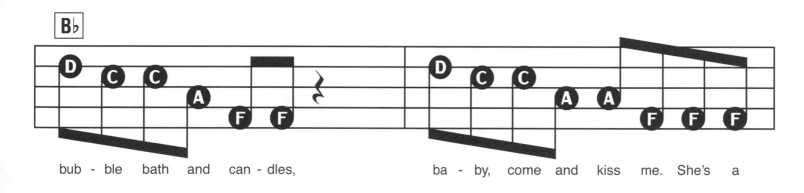

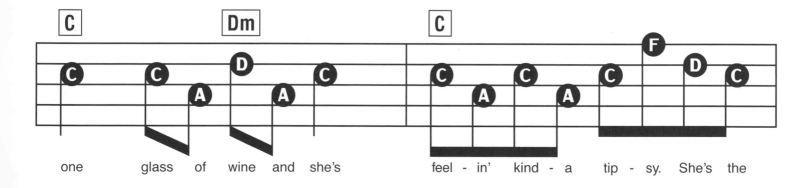

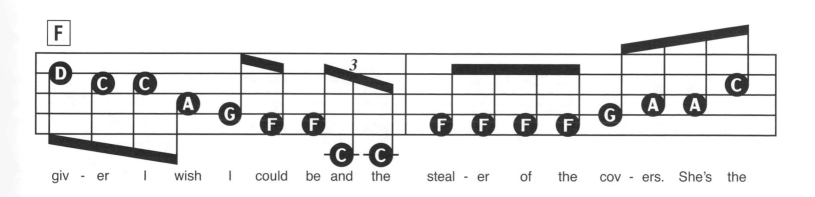

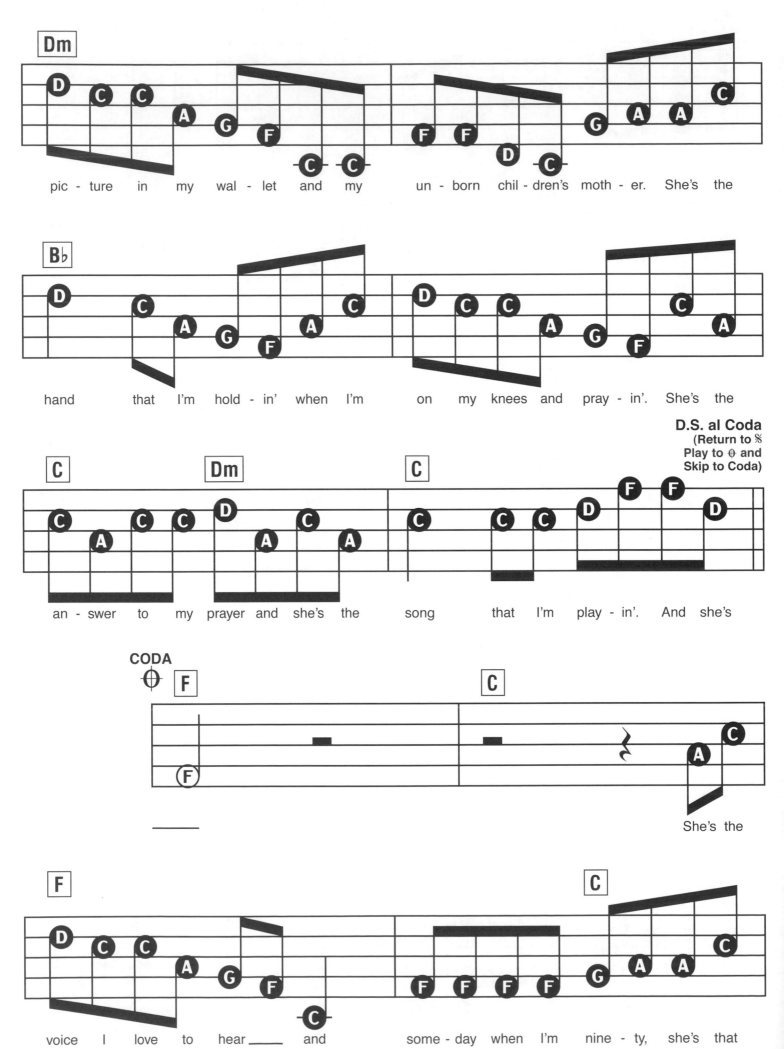

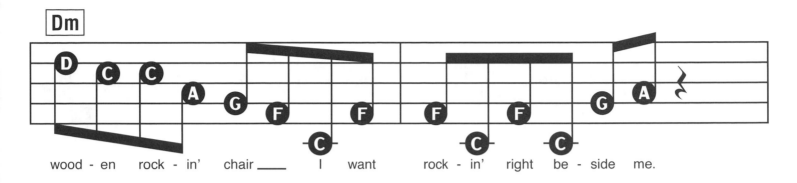

woo - den rock - in' chair ___ I want rock - in' right be - side me.

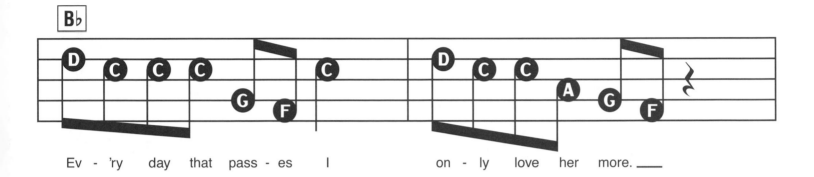

Ev - 'ry day that pass - es I on - ly love her more. ___

Yeah, she's the one that I'd lay down my own life for. And she's

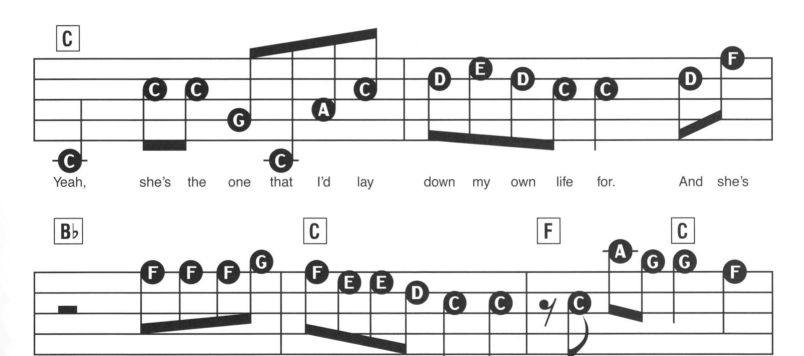

ev - 'ry - thing I ev - er want - ed, and ev - 'ry - thing I

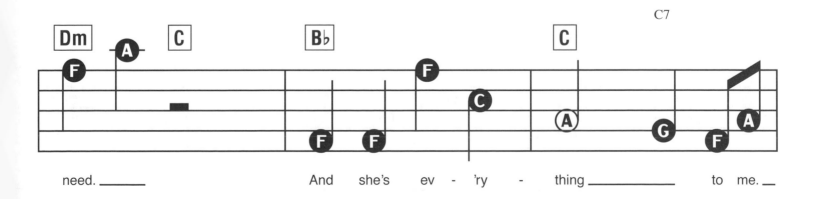

need. ___ And she's ev - 'ry - thing ___ to me. ___

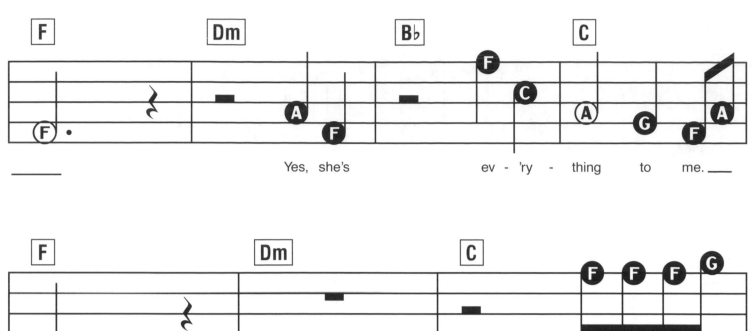

Yes, she's ev - 'ry - thing to me. ___

___ Ev - 'ry - thing I

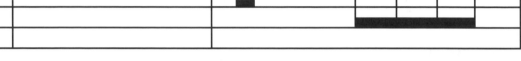

ev - er ___ want - ed

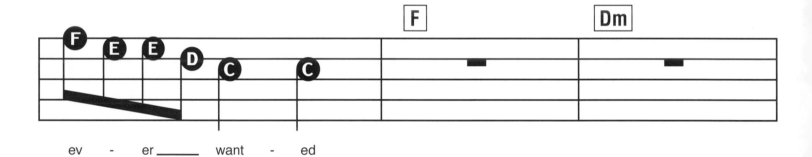

and ev - 'ry - thing I need. _____ *(Instrumental)*

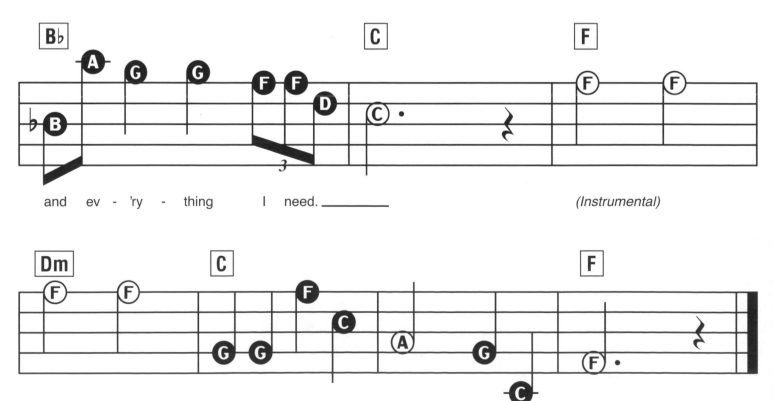

And she's ev - 'ry - thing _____ to me.

Should've Been a Cowboy

Registration 4
Rhythm: Country Pop

Words and Music by
Toby Keith

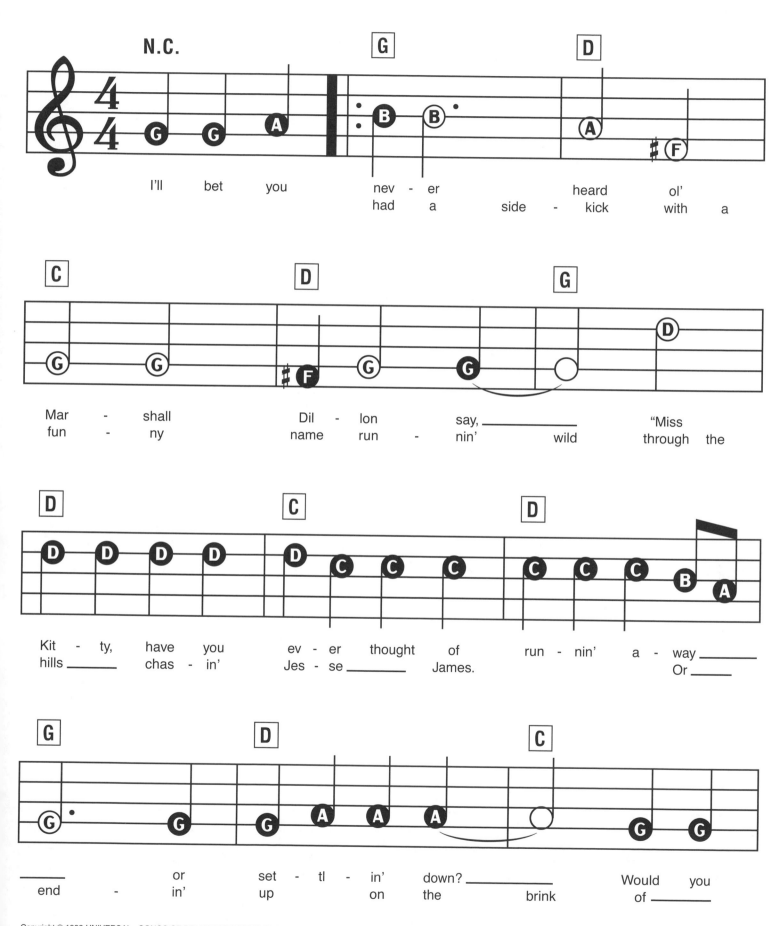

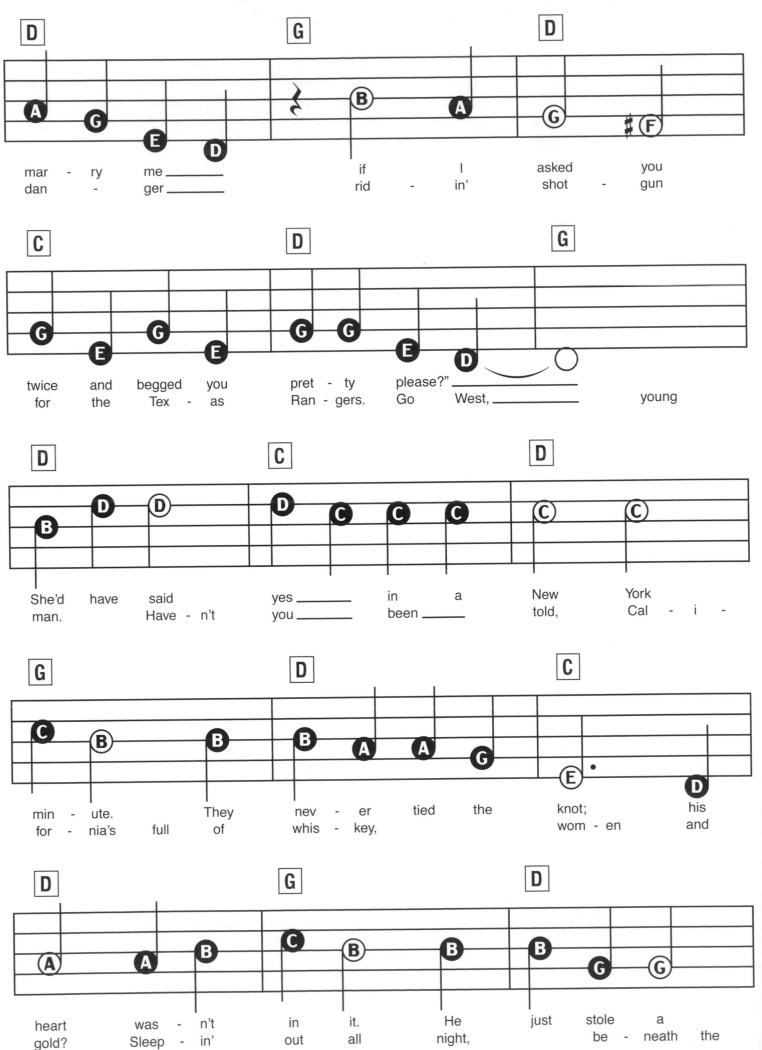

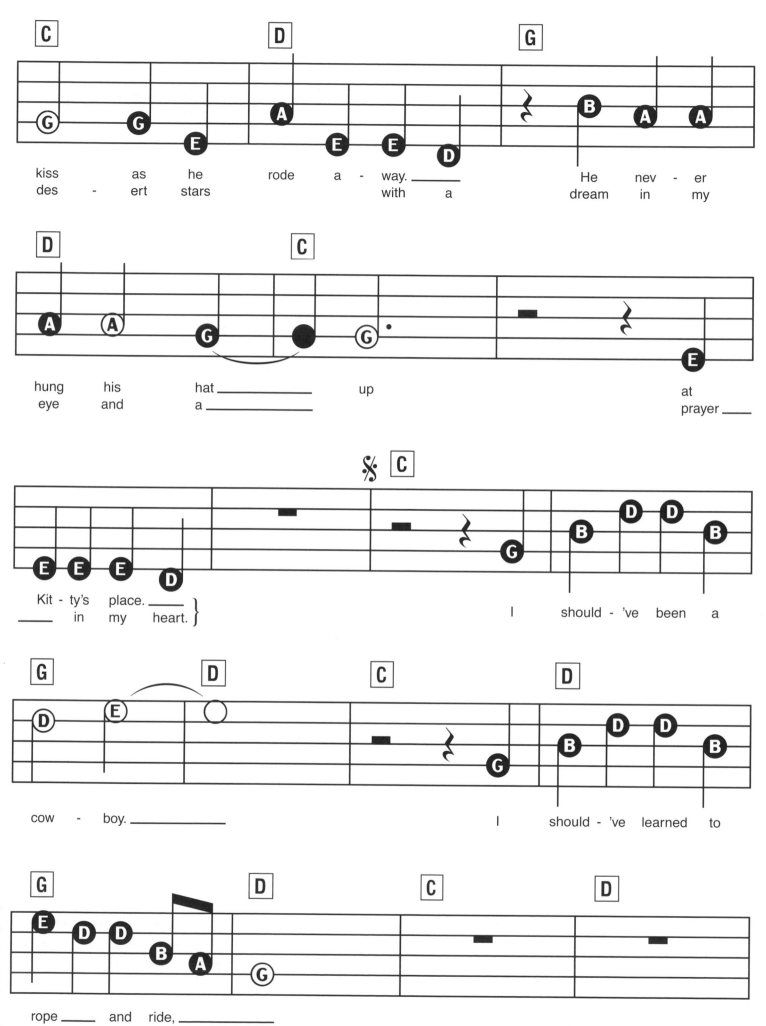

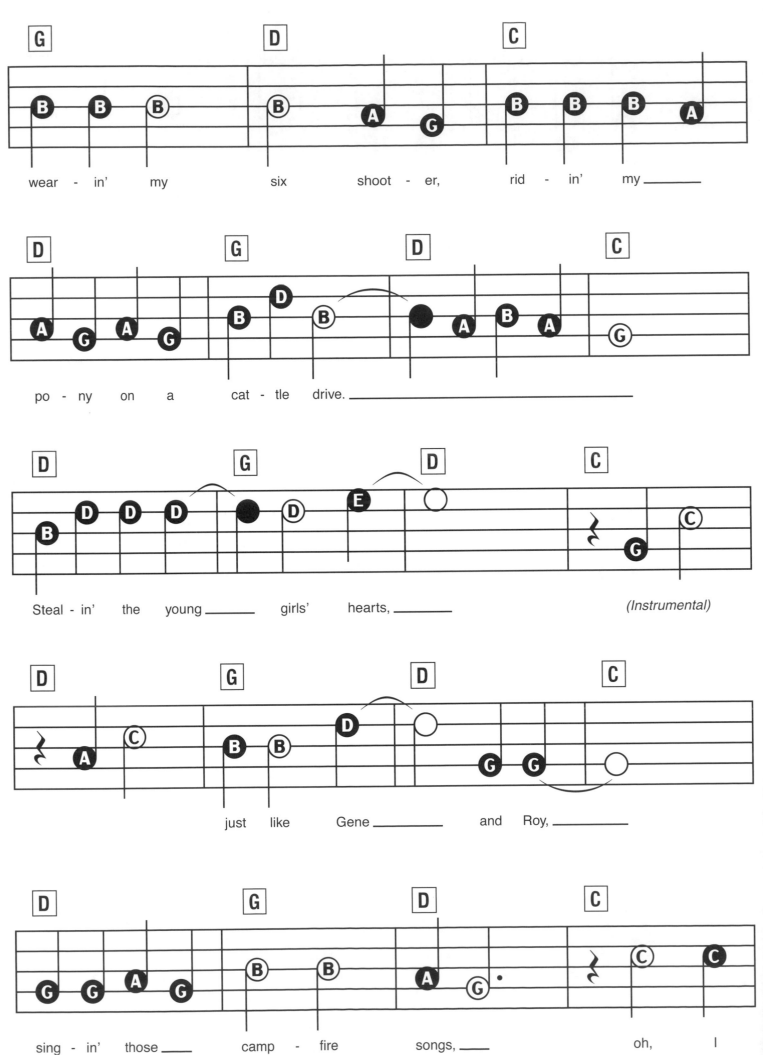

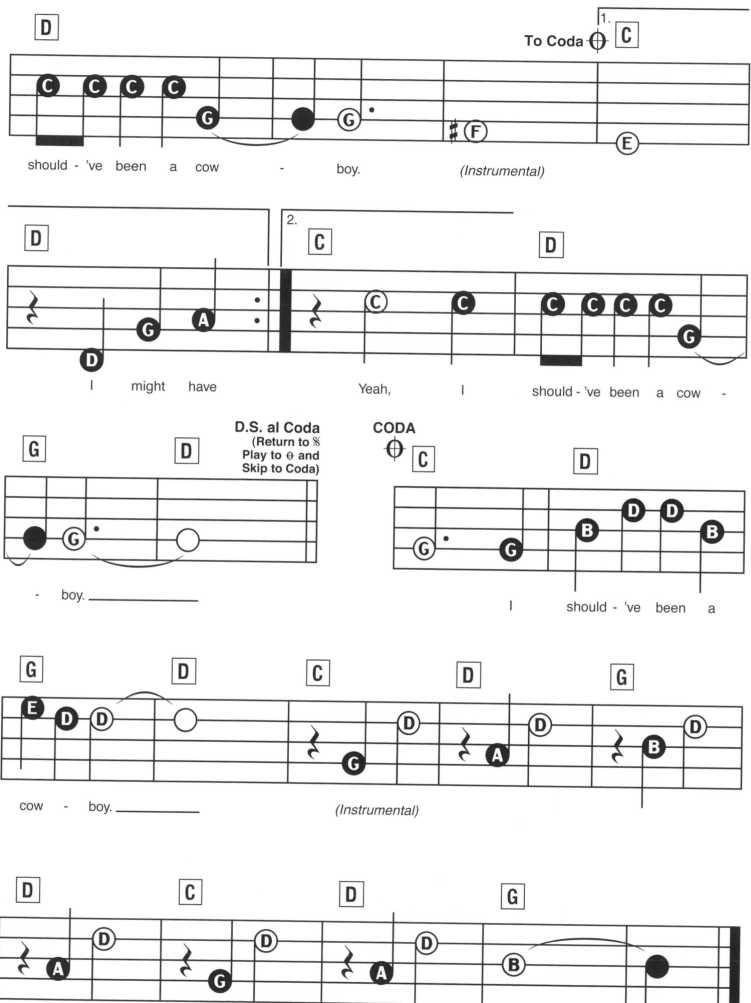

Stuck Like Glue

Registration 4
Rhythm: Country Pop

Words and Music by Kristian Bush,
Shy Carter, Kevin Griffin
and Jennifer Nettles

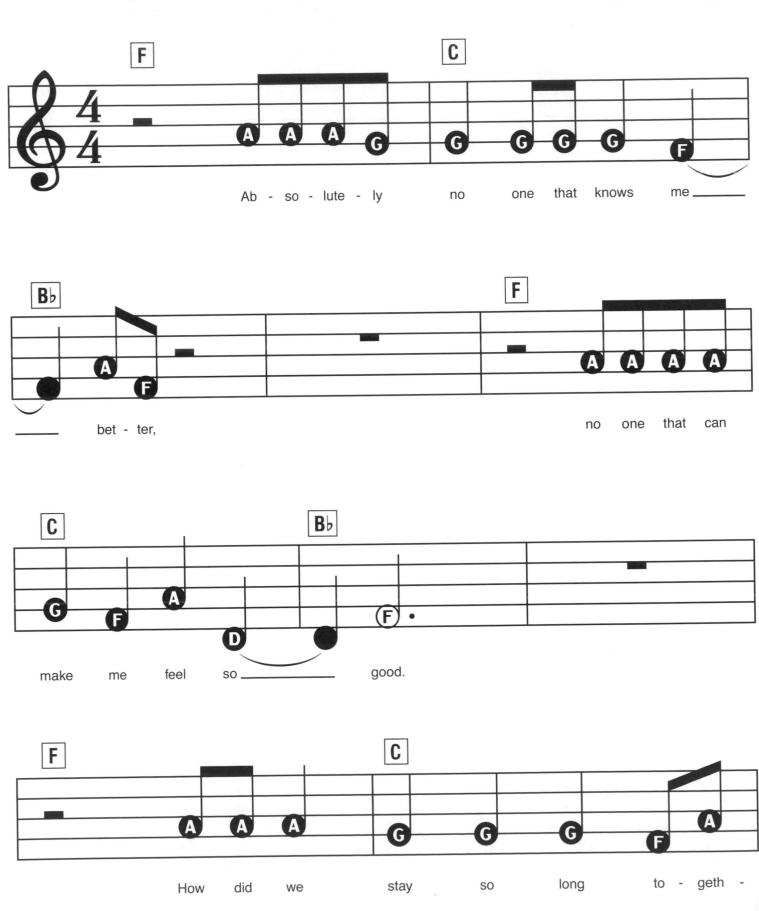

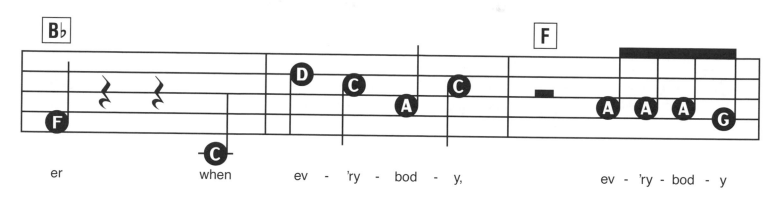

er   when   ev - 'ry - bod - y,   ev - 'ry - bod - y

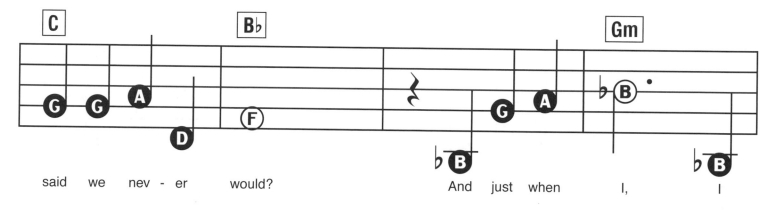

said   we   nev - er   would?   And   just   when   I,   I

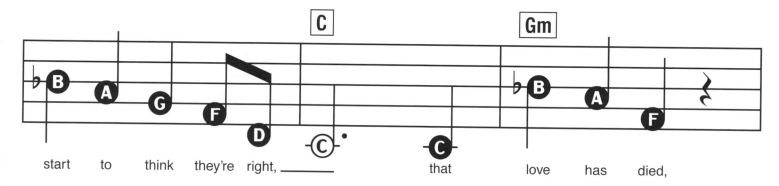

start   to   think   they're   right, _____   that   love   has   died,

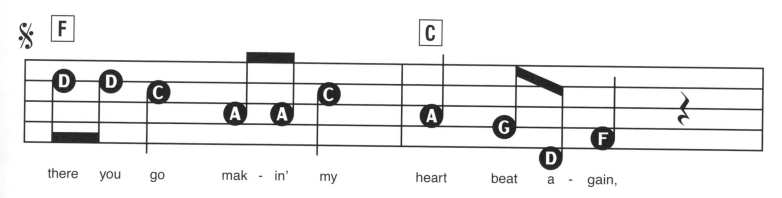

there   you   go   mak - in'   my   heart   beat   a - gain,

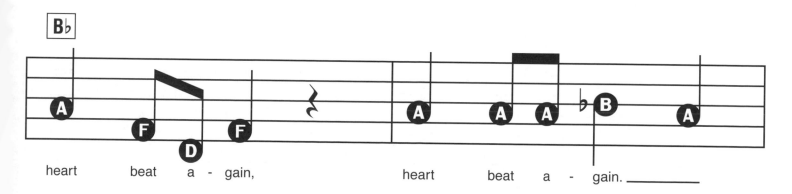

heart   beat   a - gain,   heart   beat   a - gain. _____

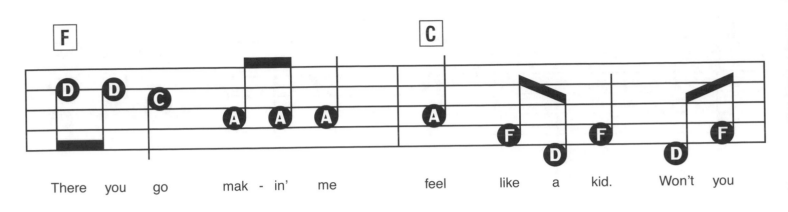

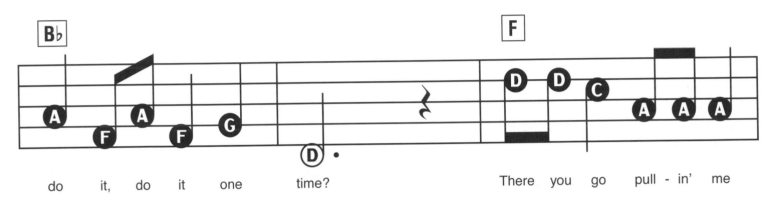

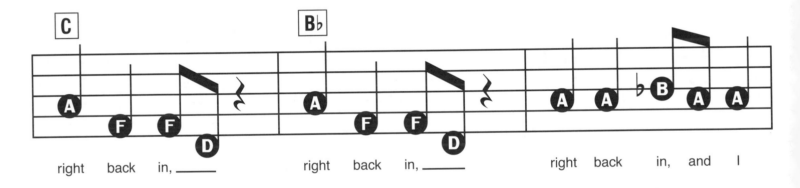

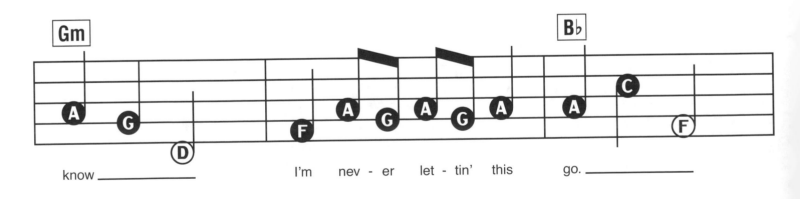

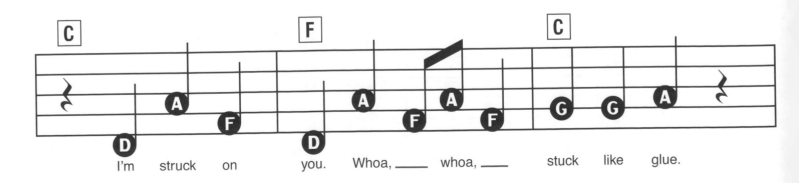

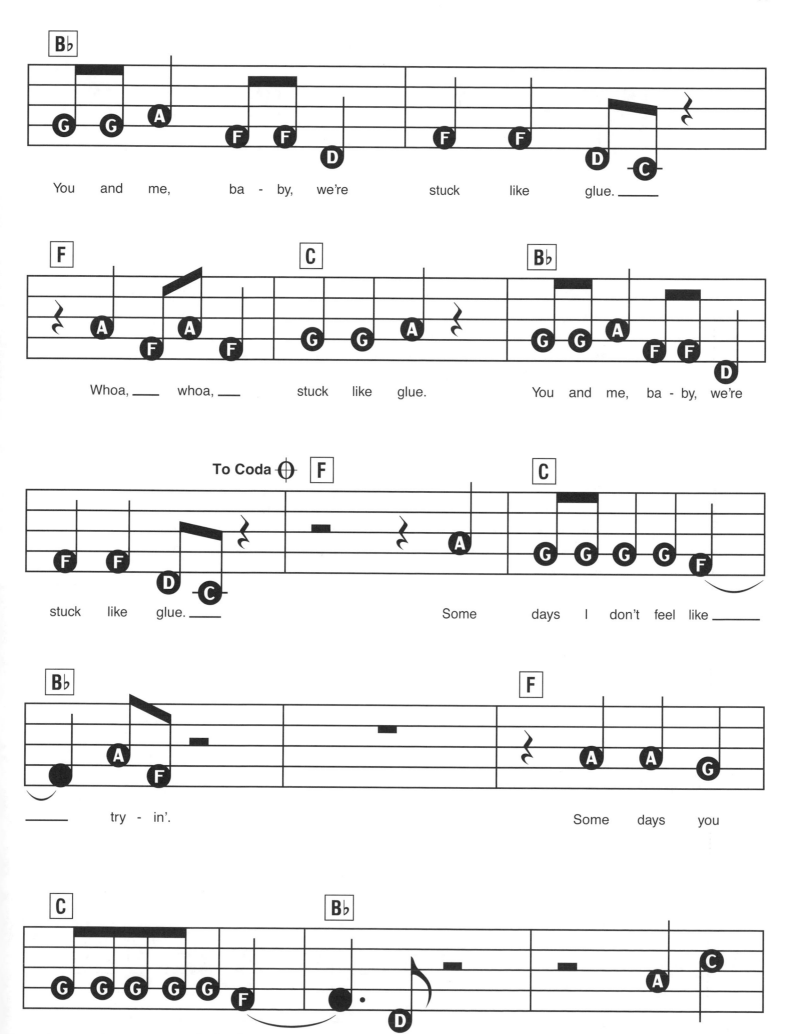

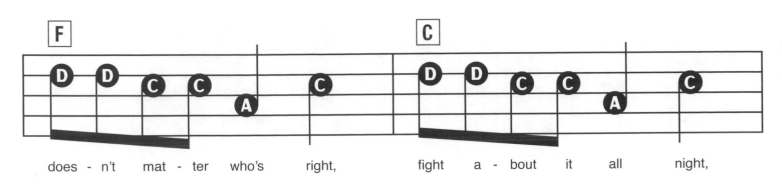

does - n't mat - ter who's right,   fight a - bout it all night,

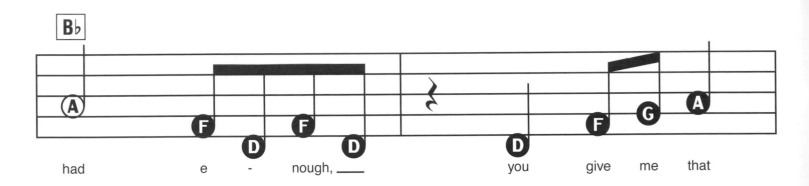

had   e - nough, ___   you give me that

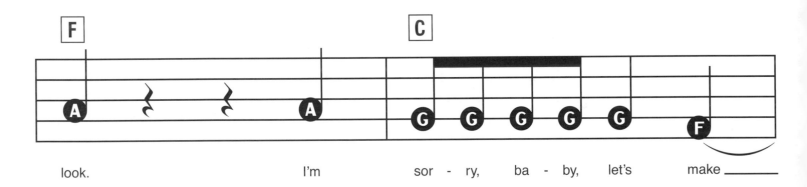

look.   I'm sor - ry, ba - by, let's make ___

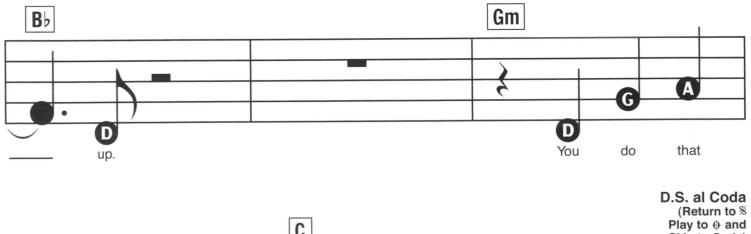

___   up.   You do that

D.S. al Coda
(Return to 𝄋
Play to ⊕ and
Skip to Coda)

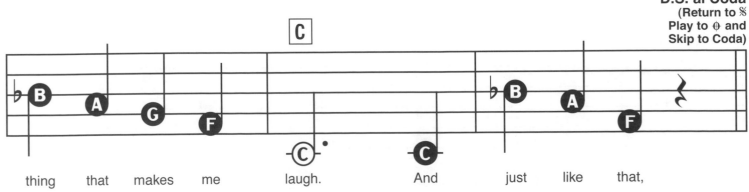

thing that makes me laugh.   And just like that,

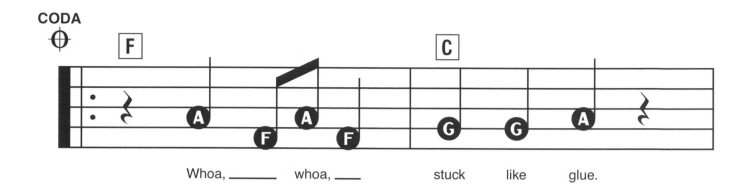

Whoa, _____ whoa, ___ stuck like glue.

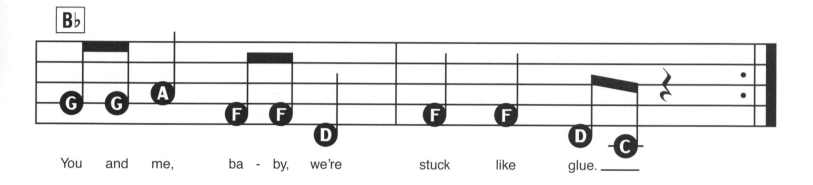

You and me, ba - by, we're stuck like glue. _____

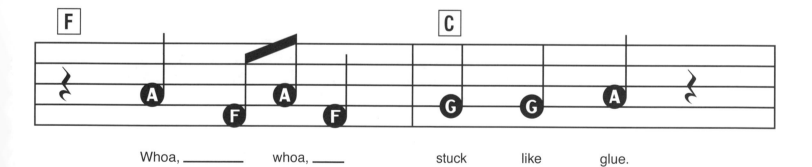

Whoa, _____ whoa, ___ stuck like glue.

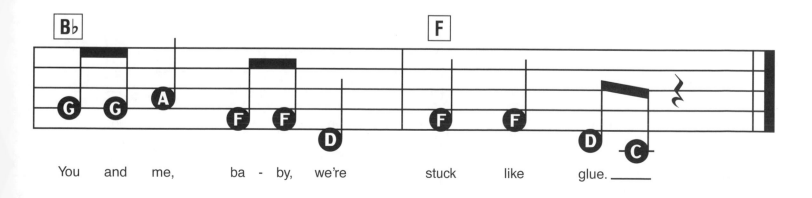

You and me, ba - by, we're stuck like glue. _____

Summertime

Registration 4
Rhythm: Country Rock or 8-Beat

Words and Music by Steve McEwan
and Craig Wiseman

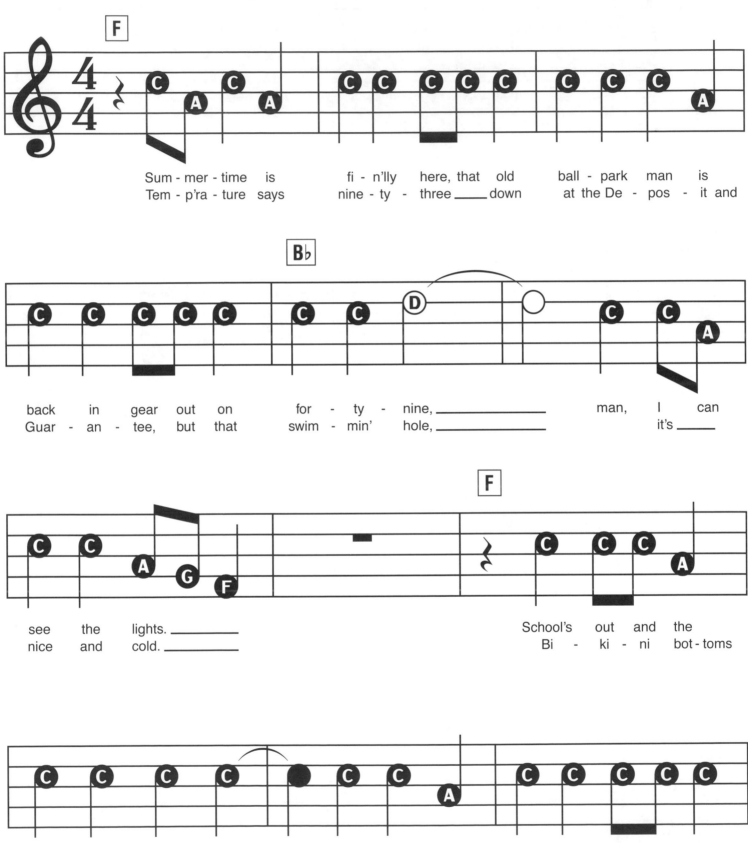

Sum - mer - time is   fi - n'lly here, that old   ball - park man is
Tem - p'ra - ture says   nine - ty - three ___ down   at the De - pos - it and

back   in   gear out   on   for - ty - nine, _____   man,   I   can
Guar - an - tee,   but that   swim - min'   hole, _____   it's ___

see   the   lights. _____   School's   out   and the
nice   and   cold. _____   Bi - ki - ni   bot - toms

nights   roll   in,   man, _____   just   like   a   long   lost   friend   you   ain't
un - der - neath,   but   the   boys'   hearts   still   skip   a   beat   when   them

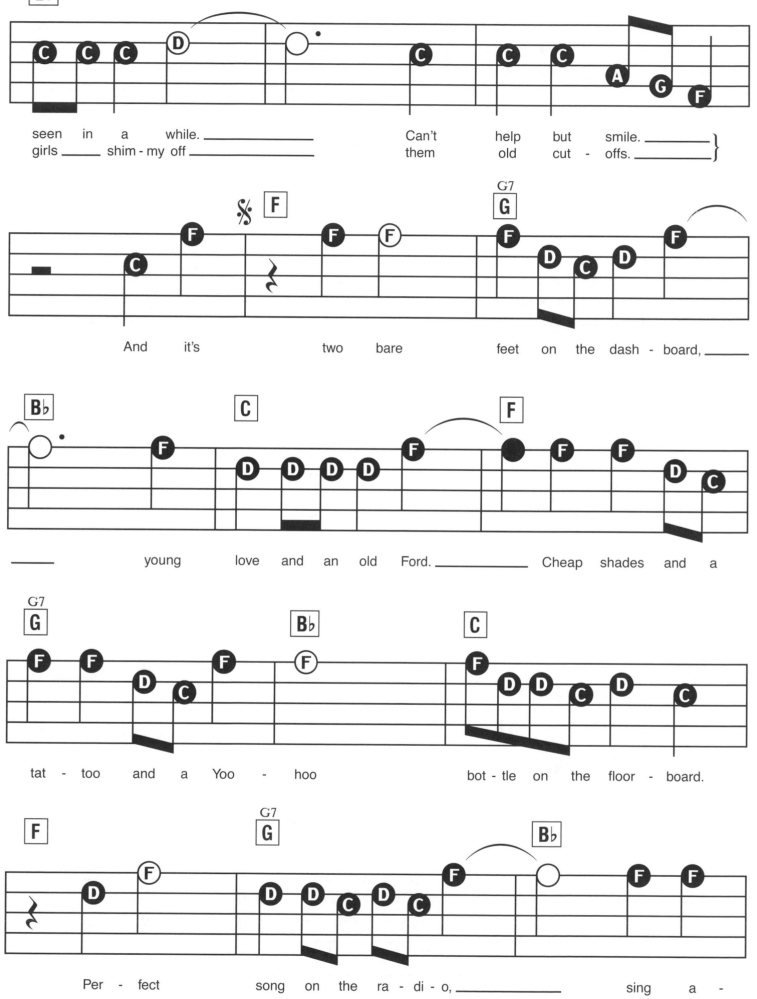

seen in a while. _____ Can't help but smile. _____
girls _____ shim-my off _____ them old cut-offs. _____ }

And it's two bare feet on the dash-board, _____

_____ young love and an old Ford. _____ Cheap shades and a

tat-too and a Yoo-hoo bot-tle on the floor-board.

Per-fect song on the ra-di-o, _____ sing a-

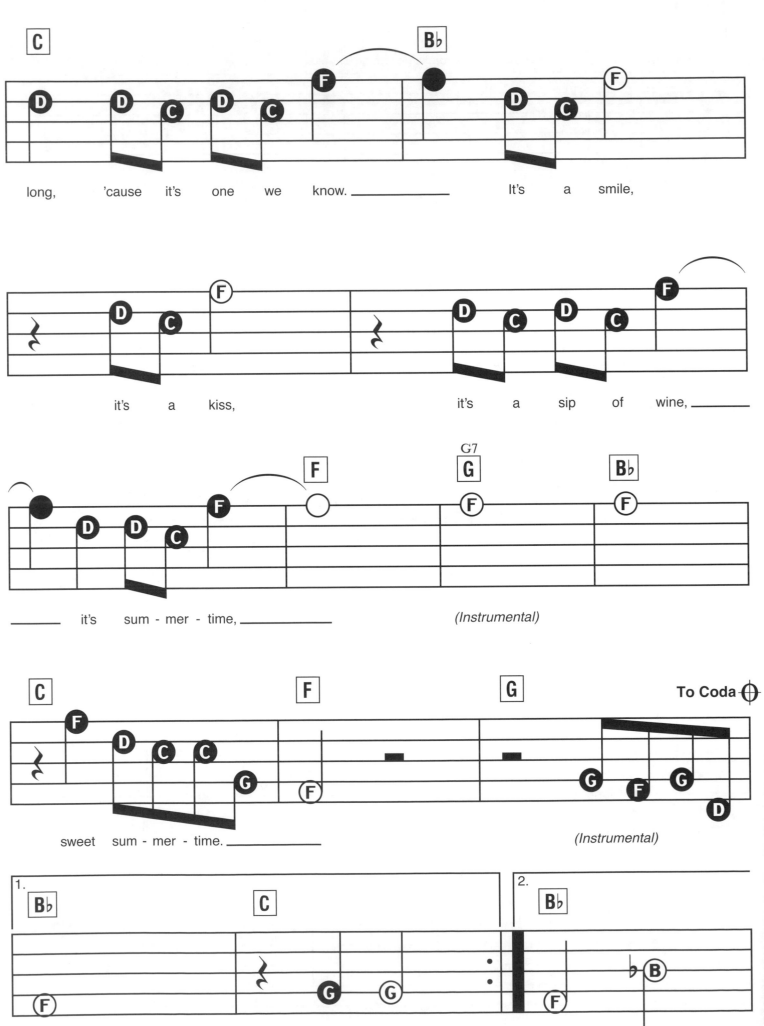

long,   'cause   it's   one   we   know. _____   It's   a   smile,

it's   a   kiss,   it's   a   sip   of   wine, _____

____   it's   sum - mer - time, _____   *(Instrumental)*

sweet   sum - mer - time. _____   *(Instrumental)*

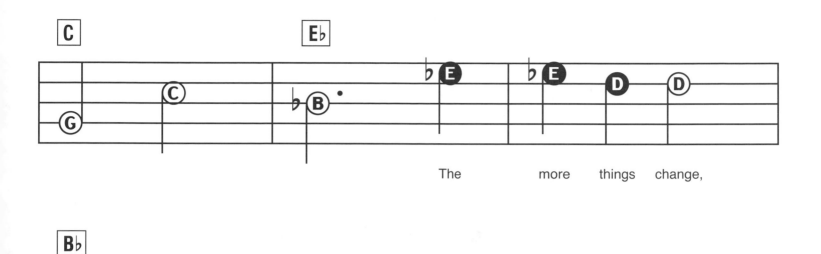

The more things change,

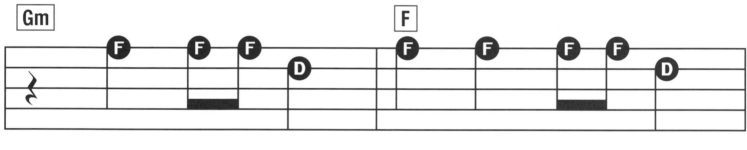

the more they stay the same.

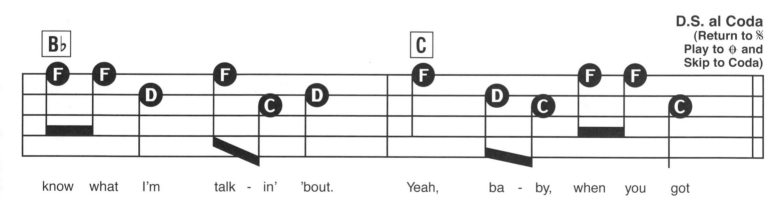

Don't mat - ter how old you are, when you

D.S. al Coda
(Return to 𝄋
Play to ⊕ and
Skip to Coda)

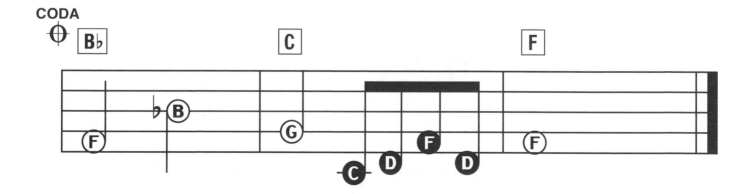

know what I'm talk - in' 'bout. Yeah, ba - by, when you got

That Don't Impress Me Much

Registration 4
Rhythm: 8-Beat or Country Rock

Words and Music by Shania Twain
and R.J. Lange

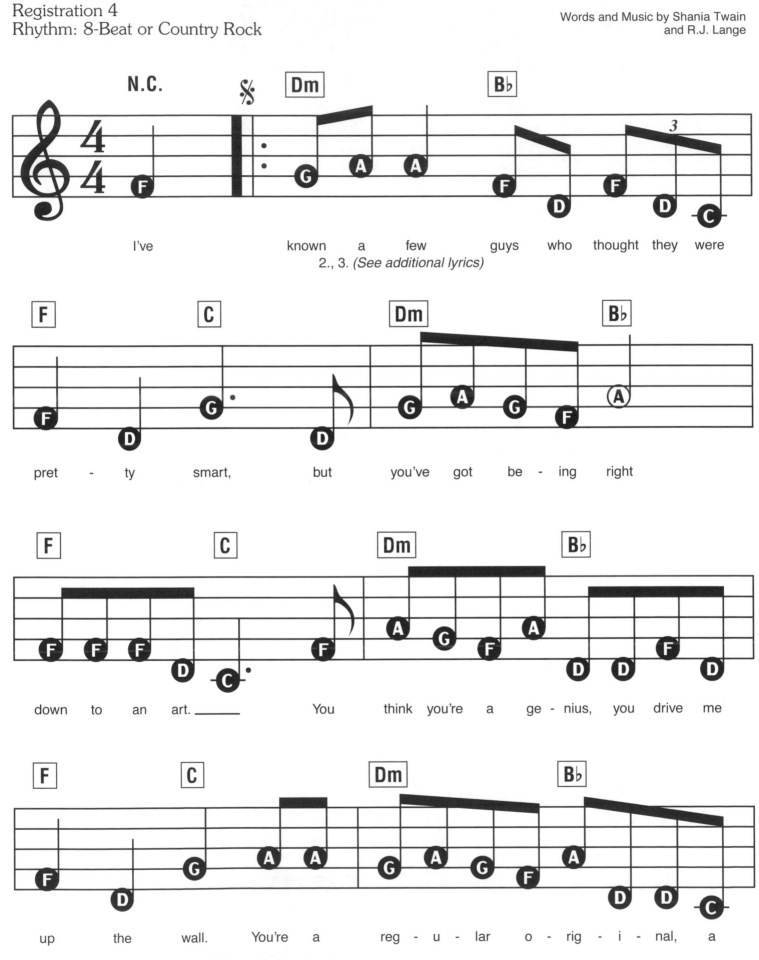

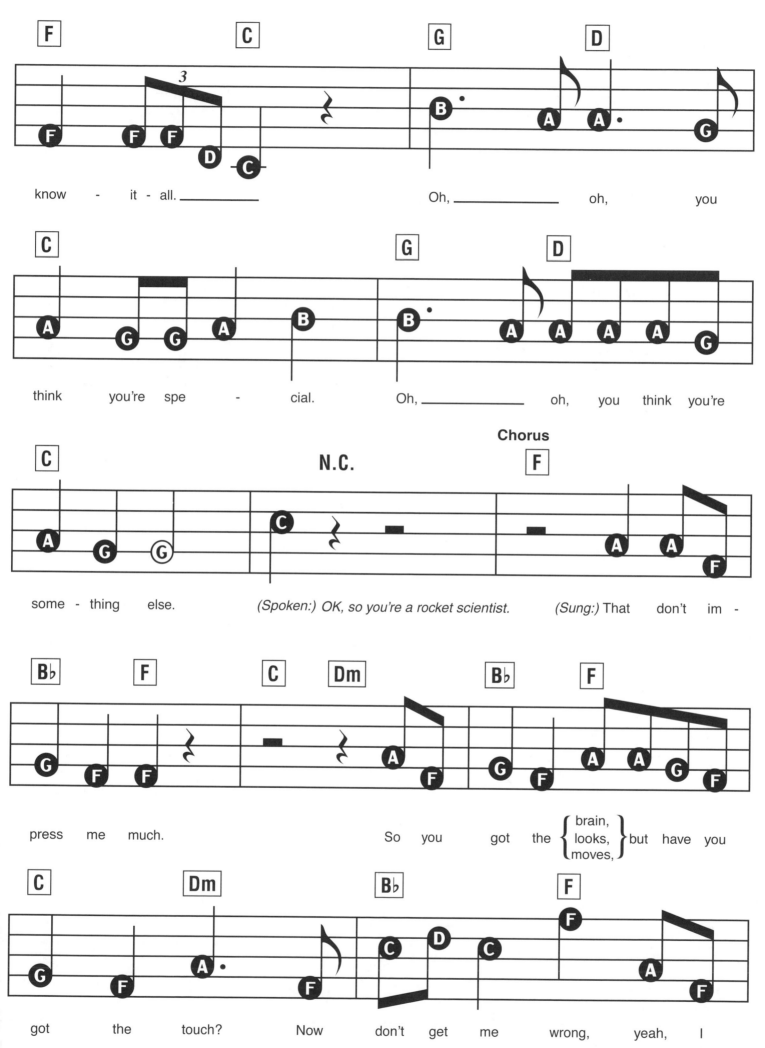

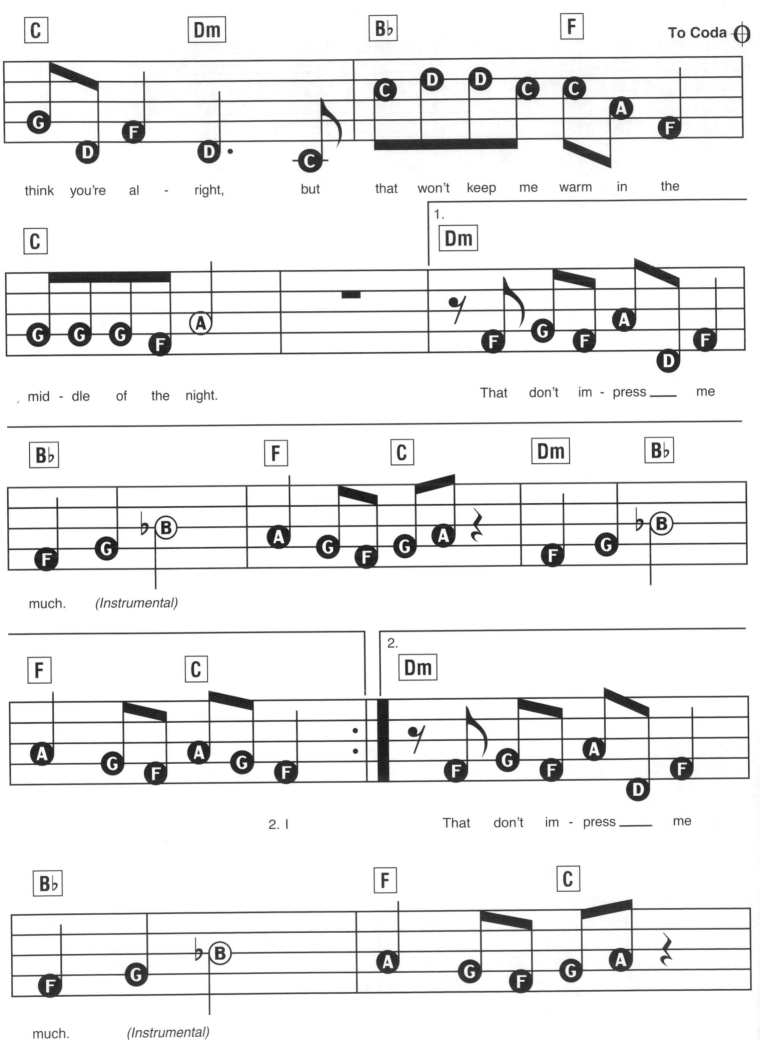

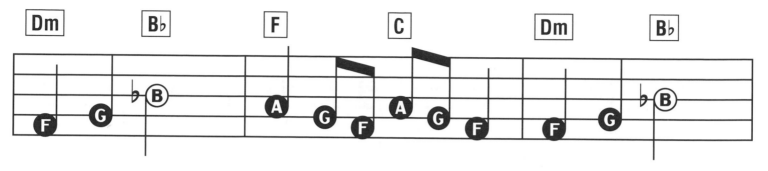

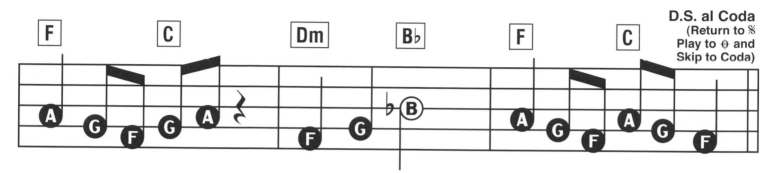

D.S. al Coda
(Return to ℅
Play to ⊕ and
Skip to Coda)

3. You're

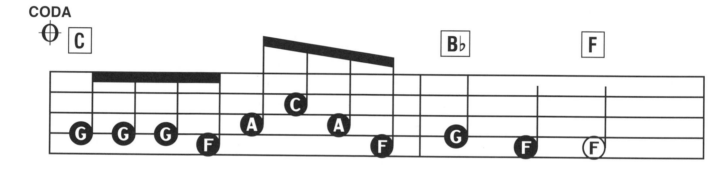

mid - dle of the night. That don't im - press me much.

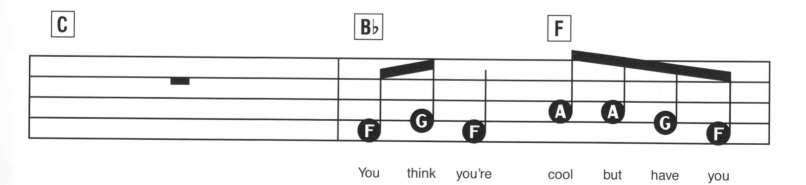

You think you're cool but have you

got the touch? Now, now don't get me wrong, yeah, I

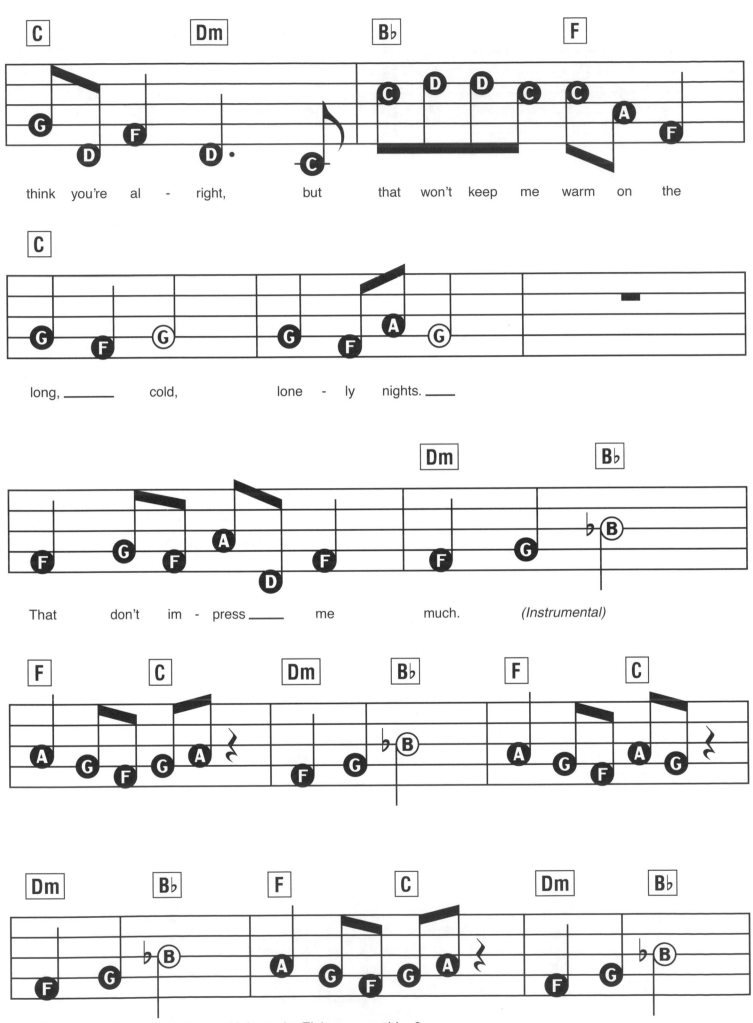

think you're al - right, but that won't keep me warm on the

long, _____ cold, lone - ly nights. _____

That don't im - press _____ me much. *(Instrumental)*

(Spoken:) *OK, so what do you think, you're Elvis or something?*

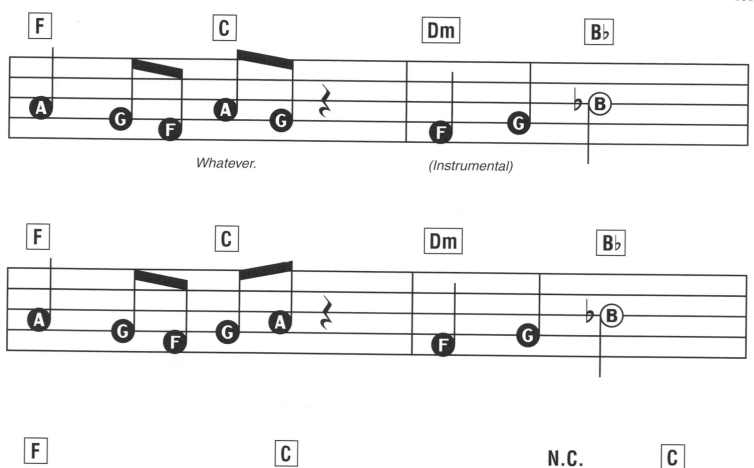

Whatever.   (Instrumental)

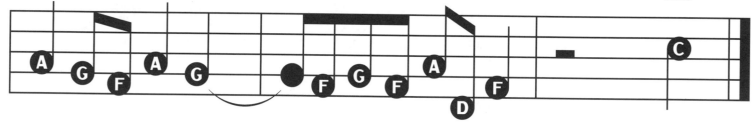

That don't im - press __ me.

Additional Lyrics

2. I never knew a guy who carried a mirror in his pocket
   And a comb up his sleeve, just in case.
   And all that extra hold gel in your hair oughtta lock it,
   'Cause heaven forbid it should fall outta place.
   Oh, oh, you think you're special.
   Oh, oh, you think you're something else.
   (Spoken:) OK, so you're Brad Pitt.
   Chorus

3. You're one of those guys who likes to shine his machine.
   You make me take off my shoes before you let me get in.
   I can't believe you kiss your car good-night.
   Come on, baby, tell me, you must be jokin', right?
   Oh, oh, you think you're special.
   Oh, oh, you think you're something else.
   (Spoken:) OK, so you've got a car.
   Chorus

Toes

Registration 4
Rhythm: Country Rock

Words and Music by Shawn Mullins,
Zac Brown, Wyatt Durrette
and John Driskell Hopkins

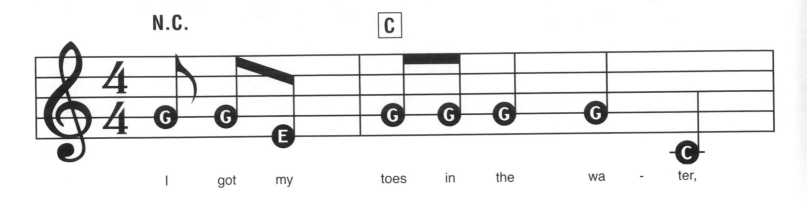

I got my toes in the wa - ter,

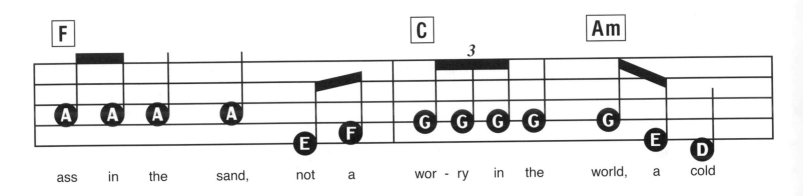

ass in the sand, not a wor - ry in the world, a cold

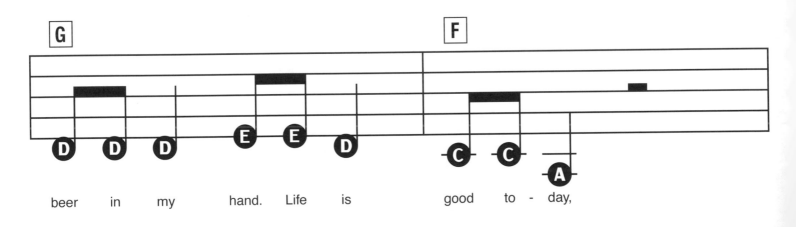

beer in my hand. Life is good to - day,

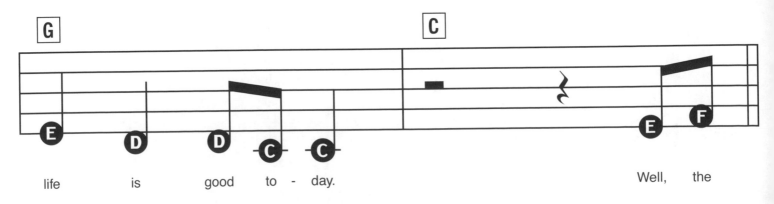

life is good to - day. Well, the

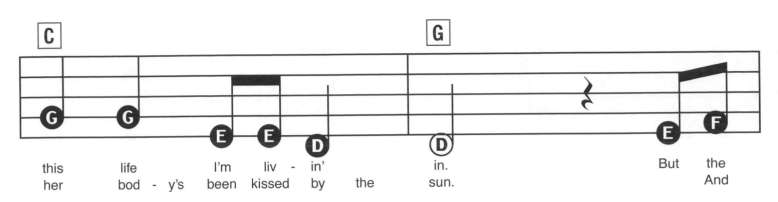

this life I'm liv - in' in. But the

her bod - y's been kissed by the sun. And

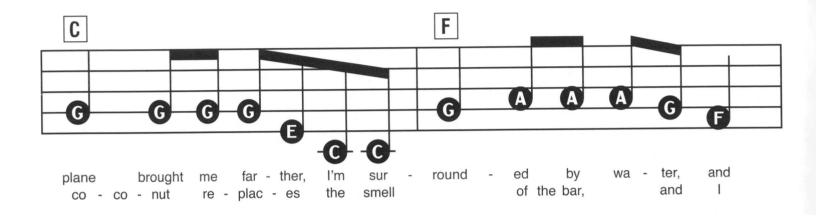

plane brought me far - ther, I'm sur - round - ed by wa - ter, and

co - co - nut re - plac - es the smell of the bar, and I

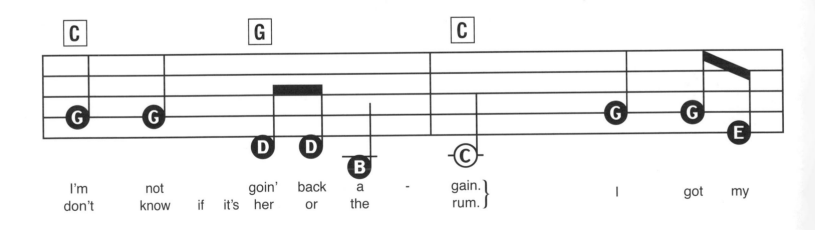

I'm not goin' back a - gain. I got my

don't know if it's her or the rum.

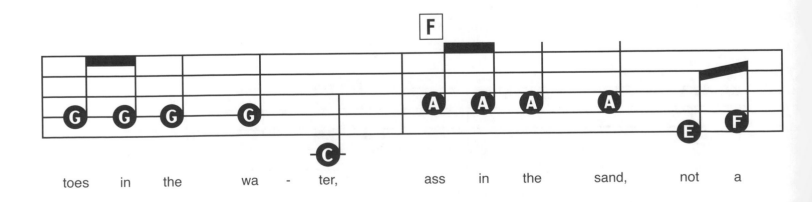

toes in the wa - ter, ass in the sand, not a

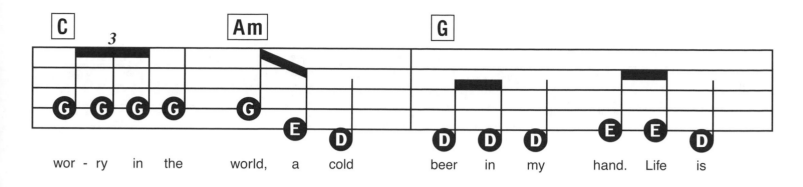

wor - ry in the world, a cold beer in my hand. Life is

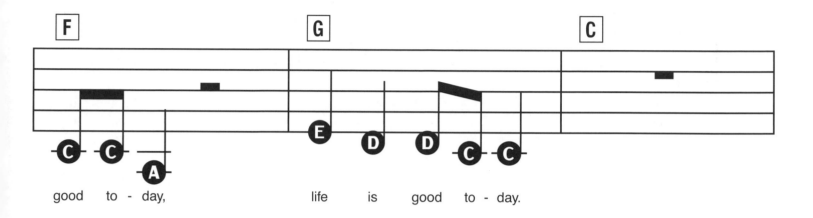

good to - day, life is good to - day.

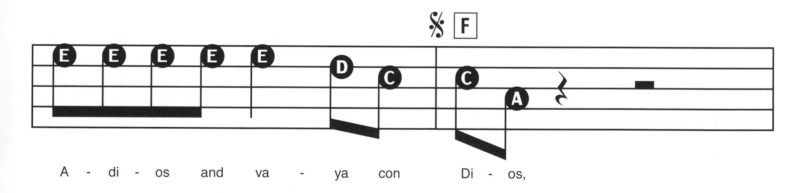

A - di - os and va - ya con Di - os,

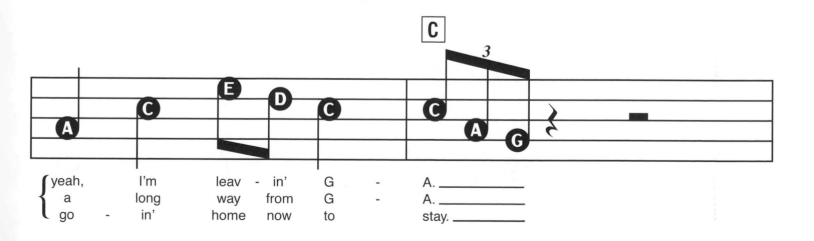

{ yeah, I'm leav - in' G - A. _____
{ a long way from G - A. _____
{ go - in' home now to stay. _____

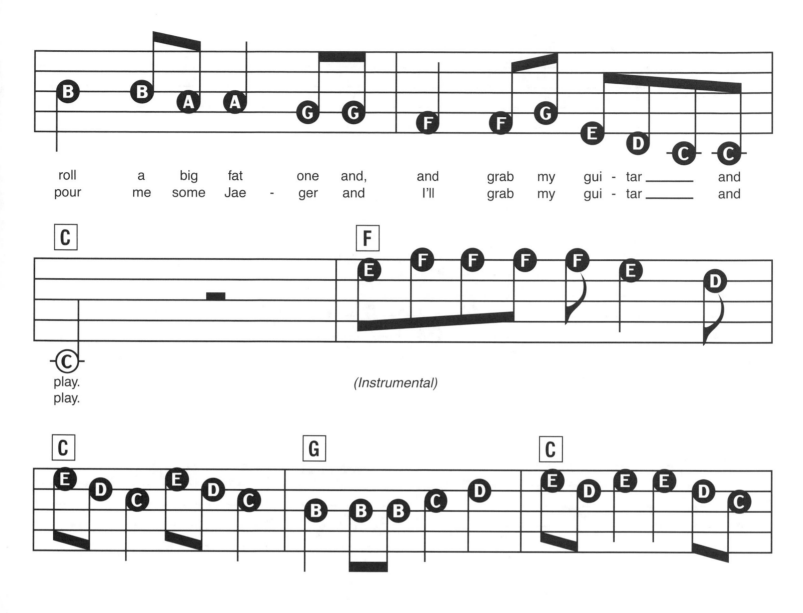

roll   a   big   fat   one and,   and   grab my gui - tar _____ and
pour me some Jae - ger and   I'll grab my gui - tar _____ and

play.
play.

(Instrumental)

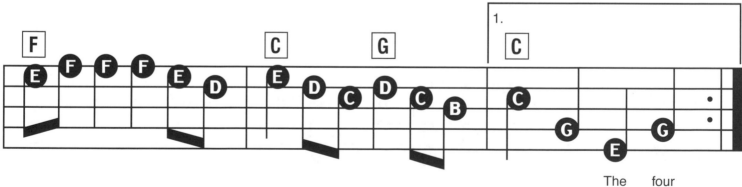

The four

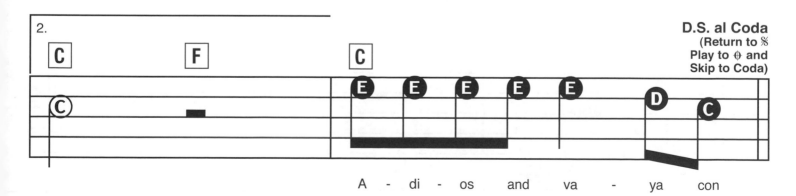

D.S. al Coda
(Return to ℅
Play to ⊕ and
Skip to Coda)

A - di - os and va - ya con

CODA

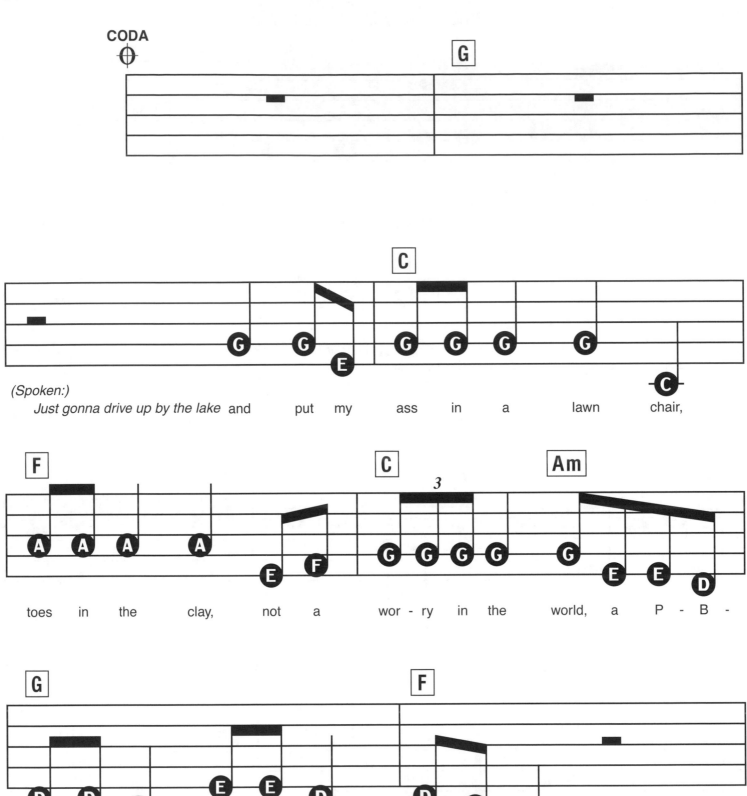

(Spoken:)

Just gonna drive up by the lake and put my ass in a lawn chair,

toes in the clay, not a wor - ry in the world, a P - B -

R on the way. Life is good to - day,

life is good to - day.

Wagon Wheel

Registration 4
Rhythm: Country Swing or Fox Trot

Words and Music by Bob Dylan
and Ketch Secor

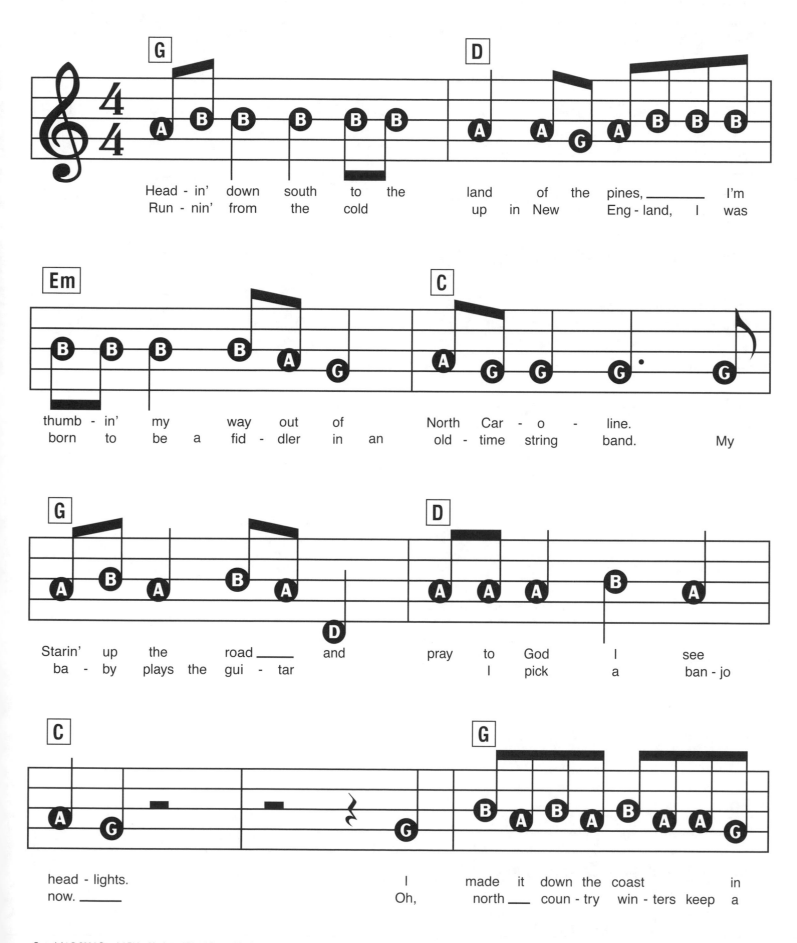

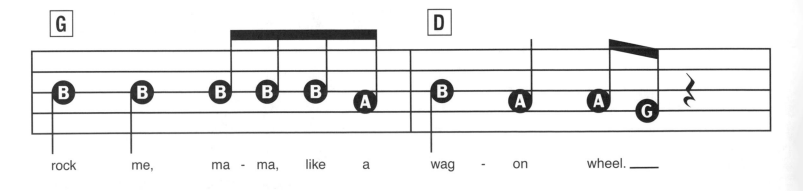

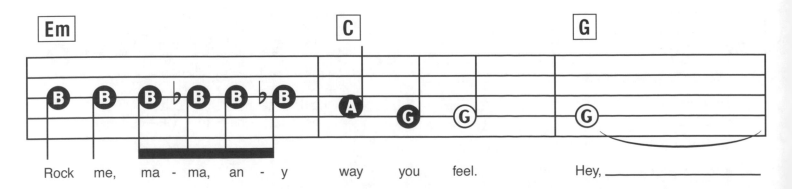

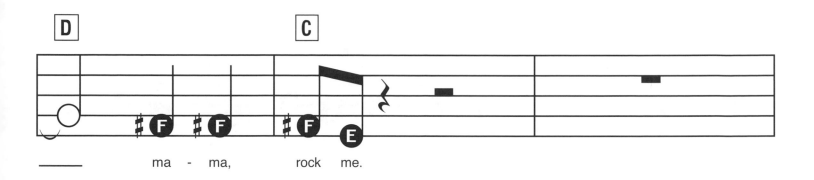

ma - ma, rock me.

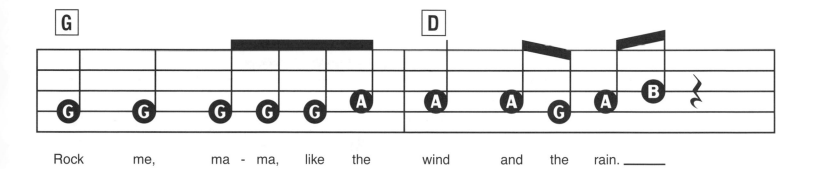

Rock me, ma - ma, like the wind and the rain. _____

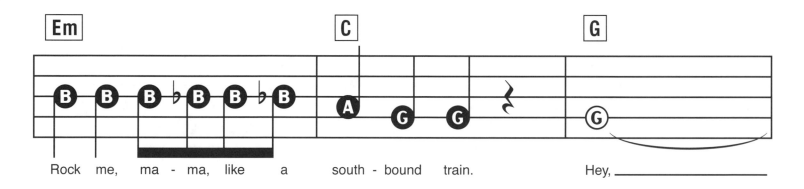

Rock me, ma - ma, like a south - bound train. Hey, _____

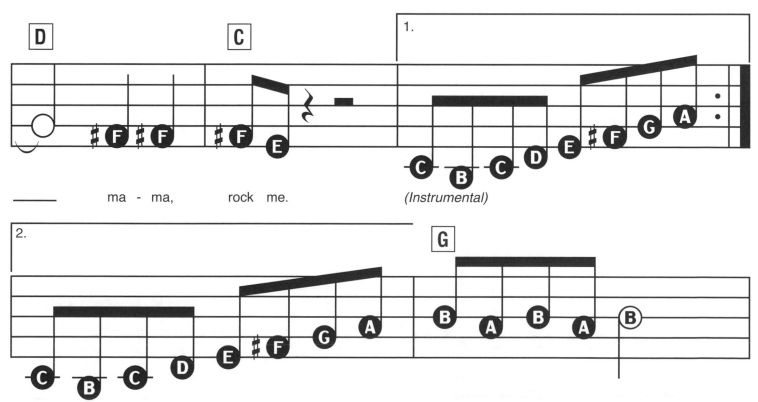

_____ ma - ma, rock me. *(Instrumental)*

(Instrumental)   Walk - in' through the South

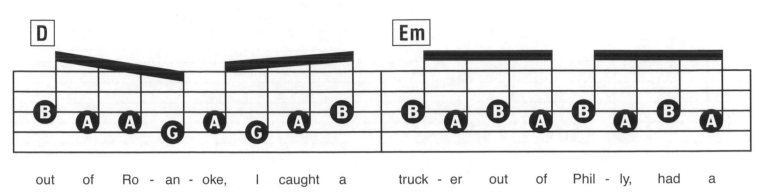

out of Ro - an - oke, I caught a truck - er out of Phil - ly, had a

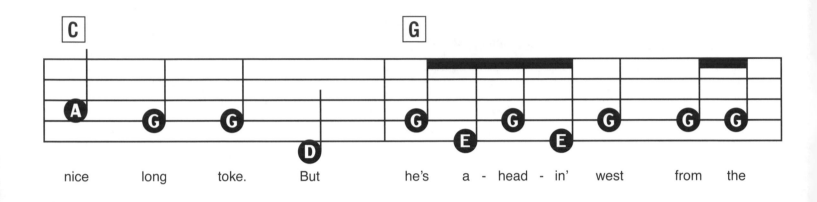

nice long toke. But he's a - head - in' west from the

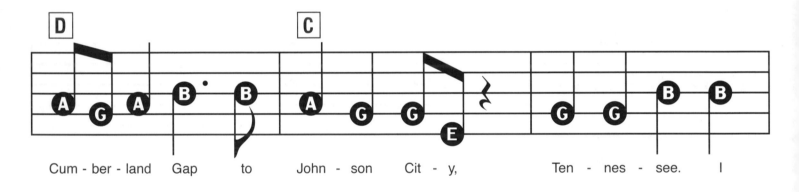

Cum - ber - land Gap to John - son Cit - y, Ten - nes - see. I

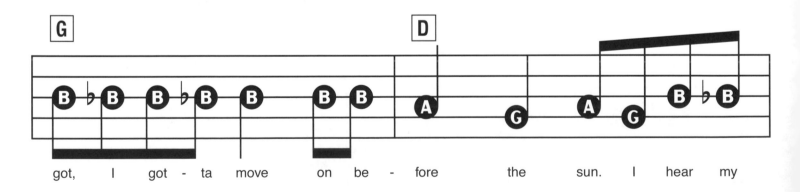

got, I got - ta move on be - fore the sun. I hear my

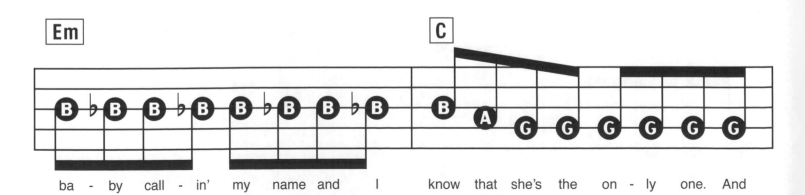

ba - by call - in' my name and I know that she's the on - ly one. And

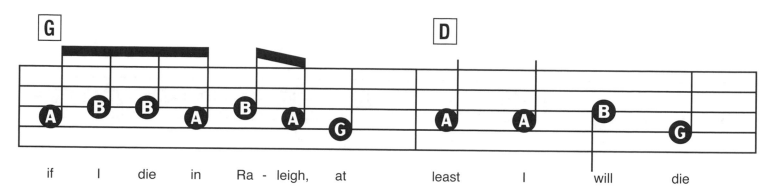

if I die in Ra - leigh, at least I will die

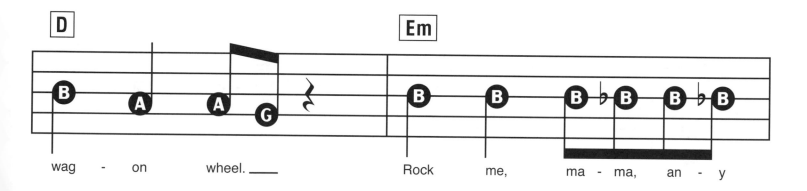

free. _____ So, rock me, ma - ma, like a

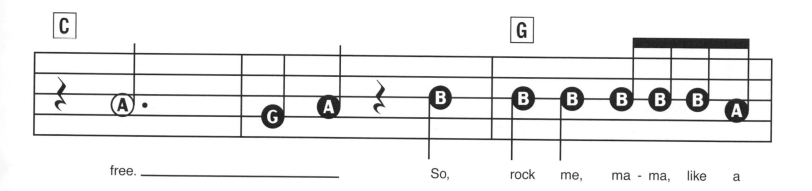

wag - on wheel. ___ Rock me, ma - ma, an - y

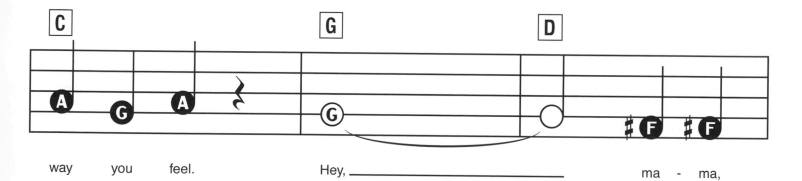

way you feel. Hey, _____ ma - ma,

rock me. Oh, rock me, ma - ma, like the

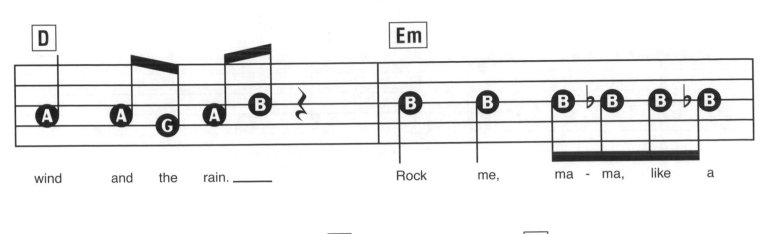

wind   and   the   rain. ____   Rock   me,   ma - ma,   like   a

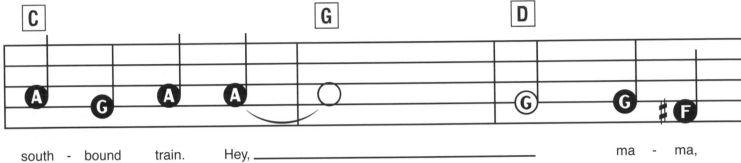

south - bound   train.   Hey, _____   ma - ma,

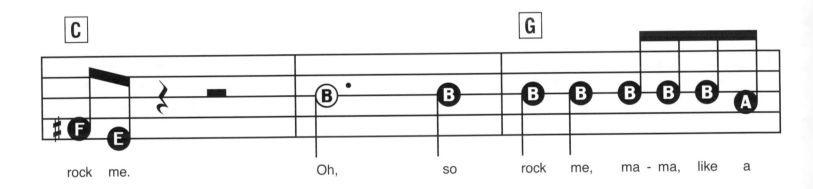

rock   me.   Oh,   so   rock   me,   ma - ma,   like   a

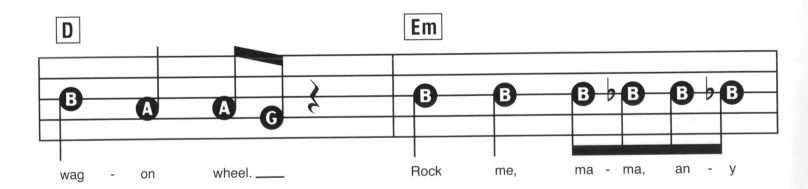

wag - on   wheel. ____   Rock   me,   ma - ma,   an - y

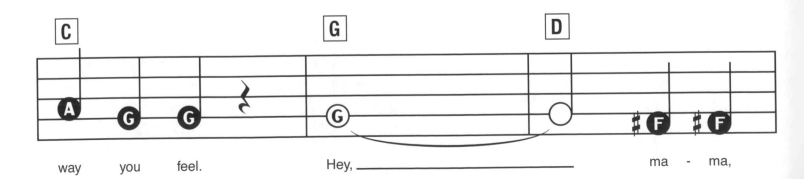

way   you   feel.   Hey, _____   ma - ma,

115

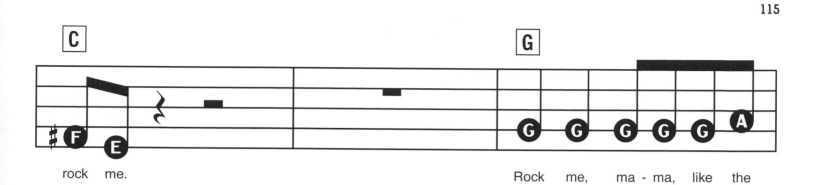

rock me.　　　　　　　　　　　Rock me, ma-ma, like the

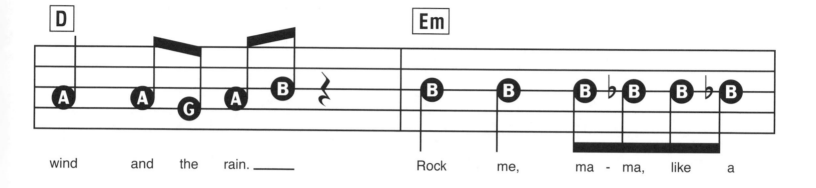

wind　and　the　rain.　　Rock　me,　　ma-ma, like a

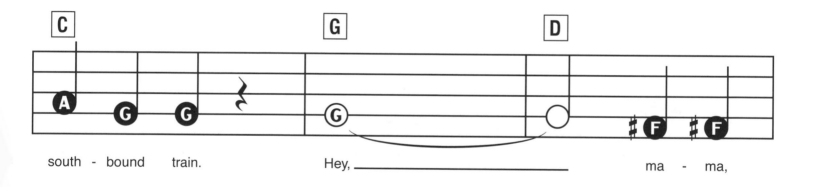

south - bound　train.　　Hey,　　　　　　　　　　ma - ma,

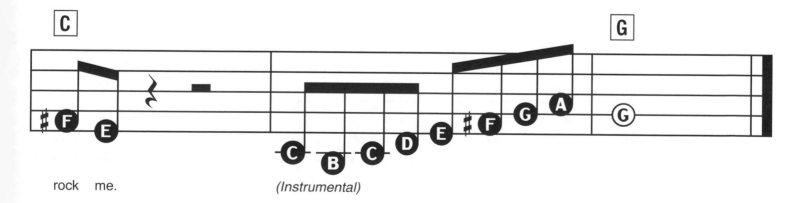

rock me.　　　(Instrumental)

Wanted

Registration 8
Rhythm: 4/4 Ballad or 8-Beat

Words and Music by Hunter Hayes
and Troy Verges

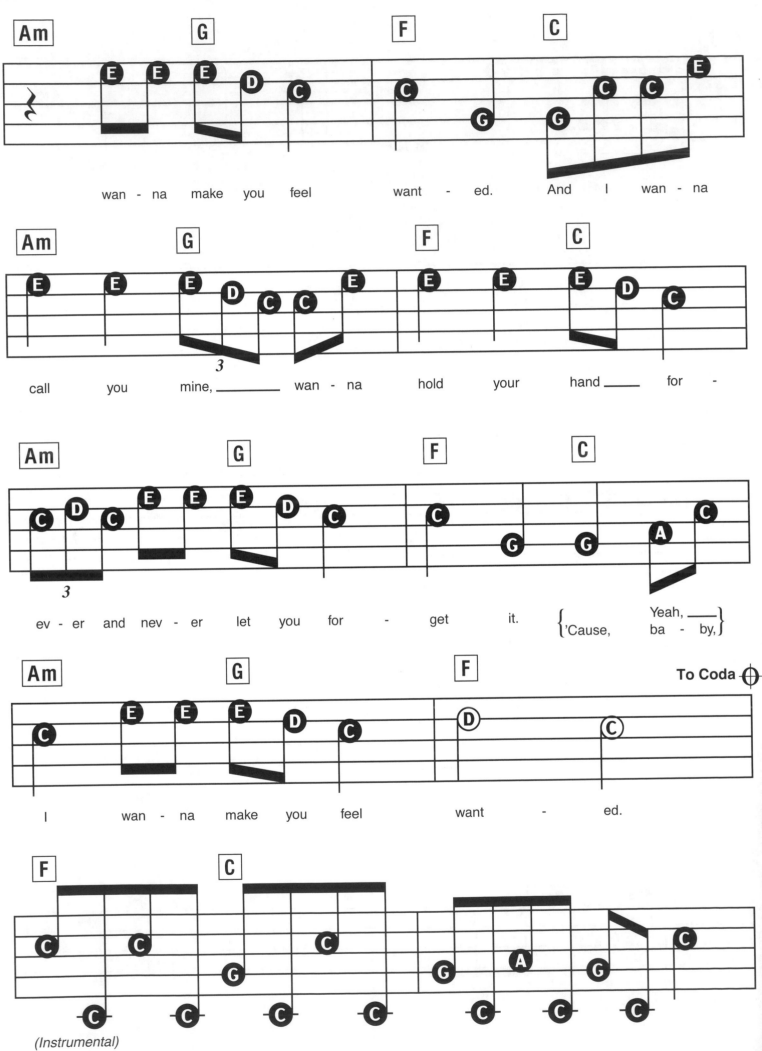

(Instrumental)

120

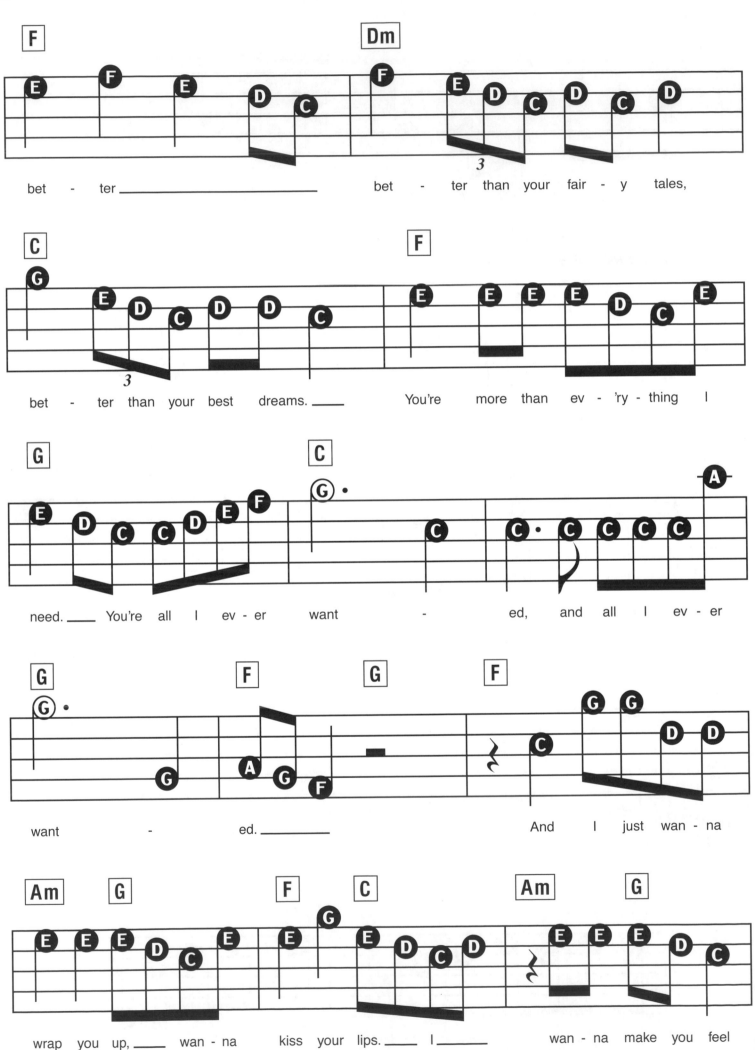

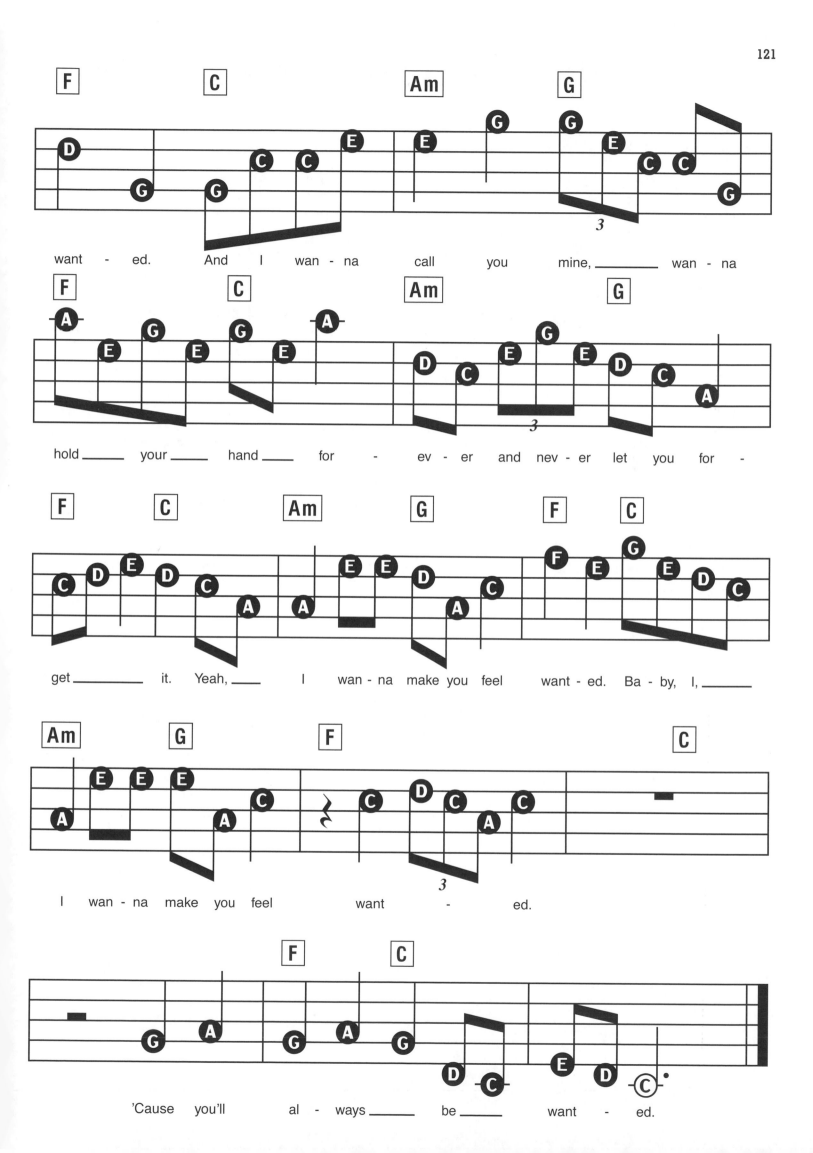

What Hurts the Most

Registration 3
Rhythm: 4/4 Ballad or 8-Beat

Words and Music by Steve Robson
and Jeffrey Steele

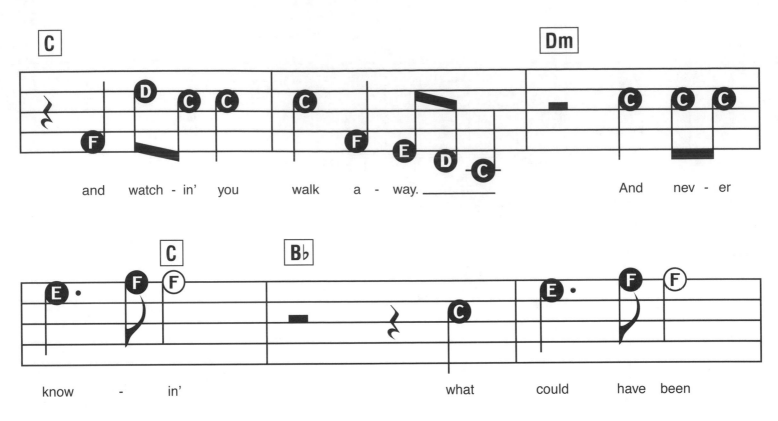

and watch - in' you walk a - way. _____ And nev - er

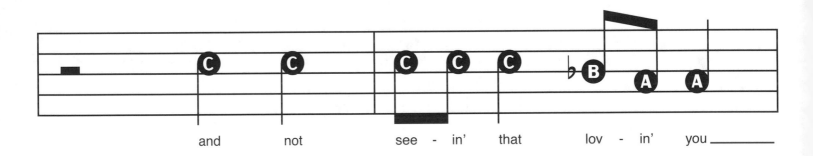

know - in' what could have been

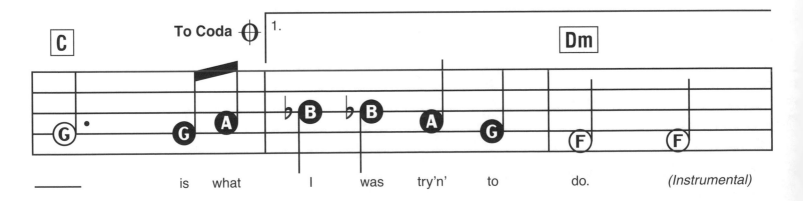

and not see - in' that lov - in' you _____

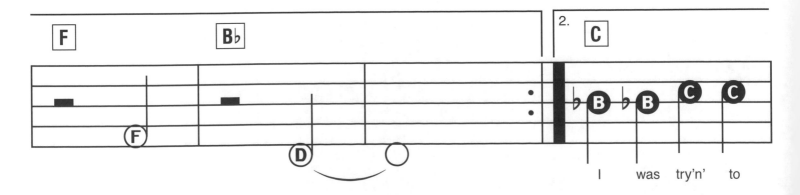

_____ is what I was try'n' to do. *(Instrumental)*

I was try'n' to

D.S. al Coda
(Return to ℅
Play to ⊕ and
Skip to Coda)

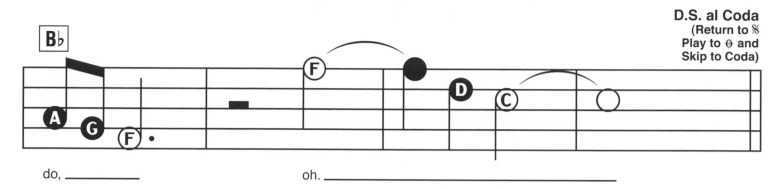

do, _____   oh. _____

CODA

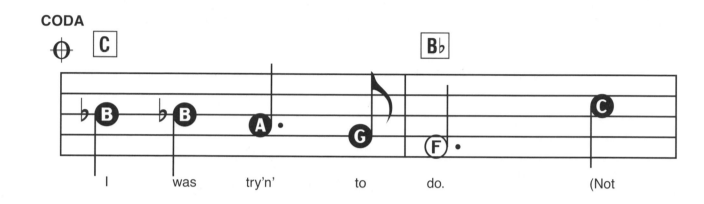

I   was   try'n'   to   do.   (Not

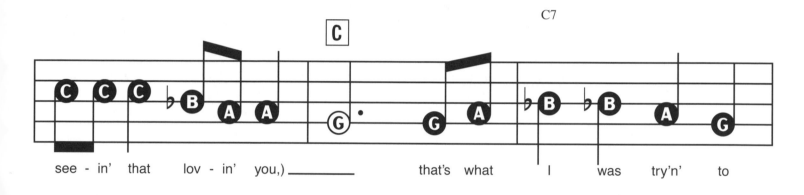

see - in' that   lov - in' you,) _____   that's what   I   was   try'n'   to

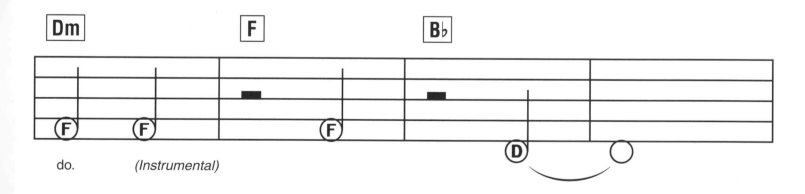

do.   (Instrumental)

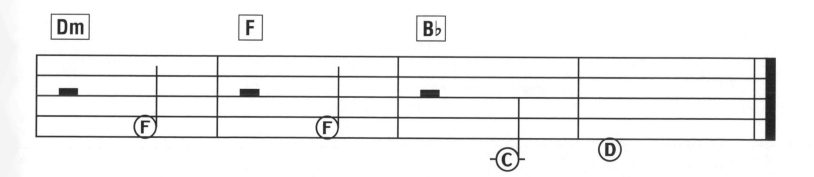

Wide Open Spaces

Registration 2
Rhythm: 8-Beat or Country Pop

Words and Music by
Susan Gibson

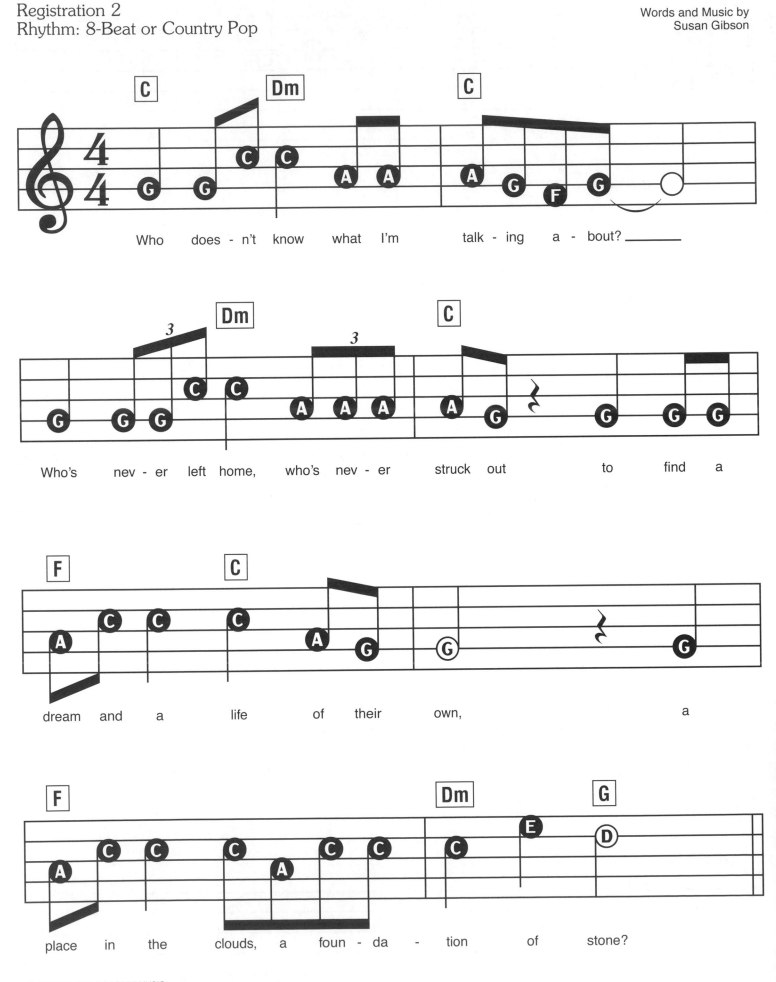

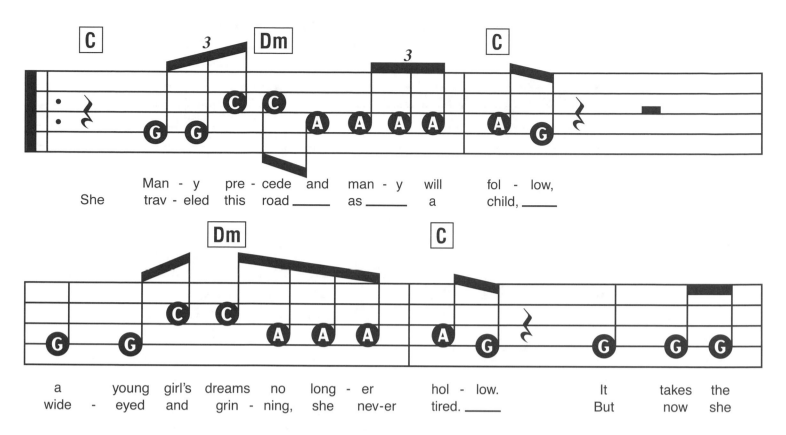

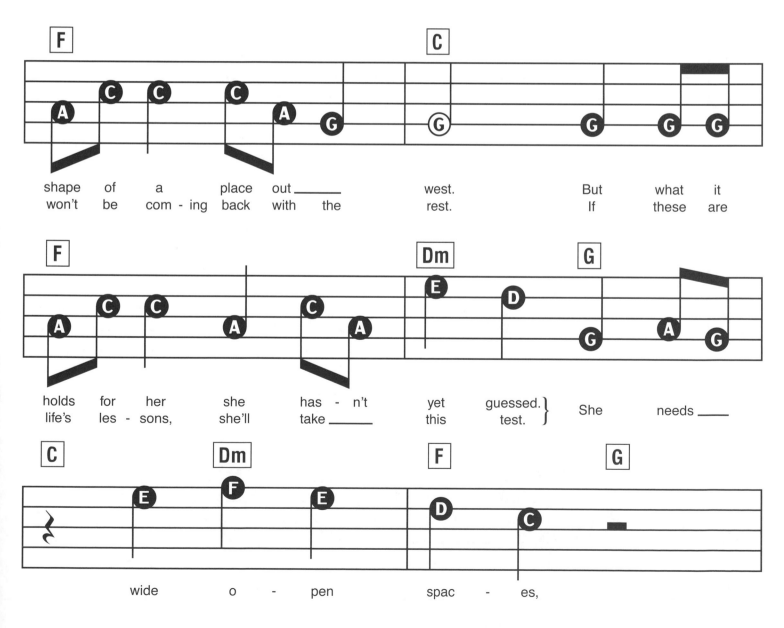

128

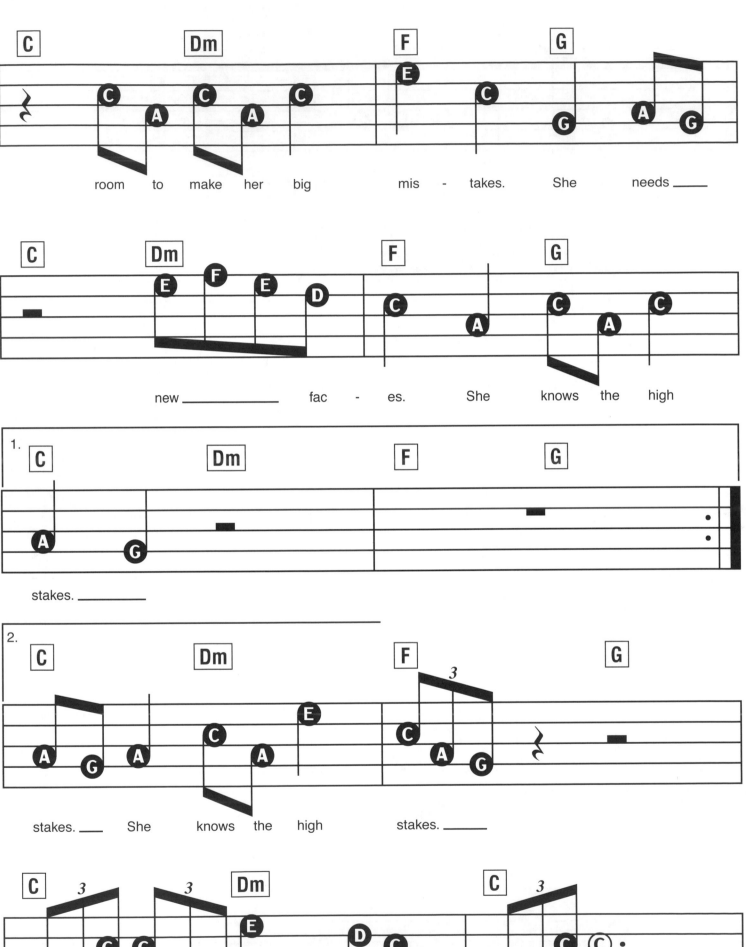

room to make her big mis - takes. She needs _____

new _____ fac - es. She knows the high

1.

stakes. _____

2.

stakes. ___ She knows the high stakes. _____

(Instrumental)

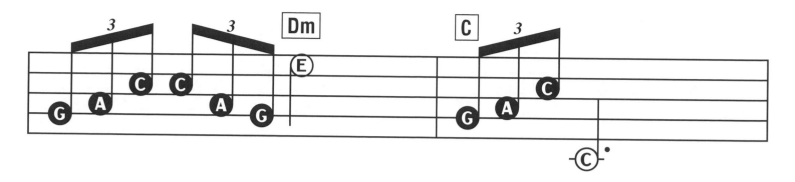

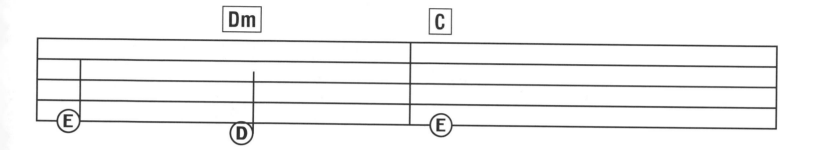

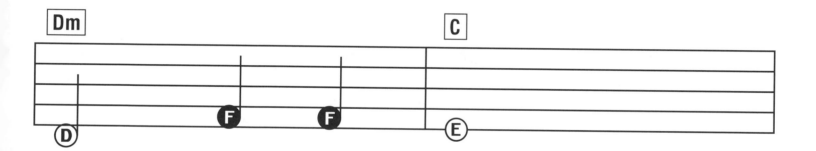

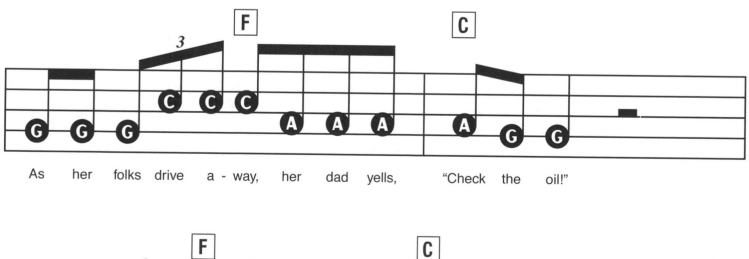

As her folks drive a - way, her dad yells, "Check the oil!"

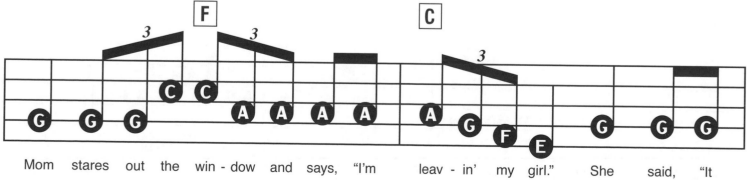

Mom stares out the win - dow and says, "I'm leav - in' my girl." She said, "It

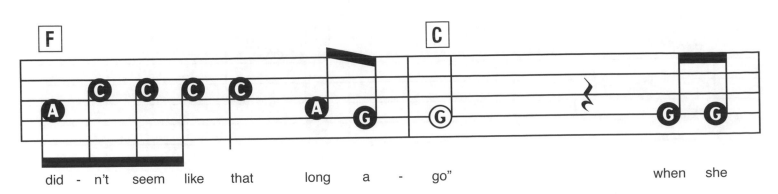

did - n't seem like that long a - go" when she

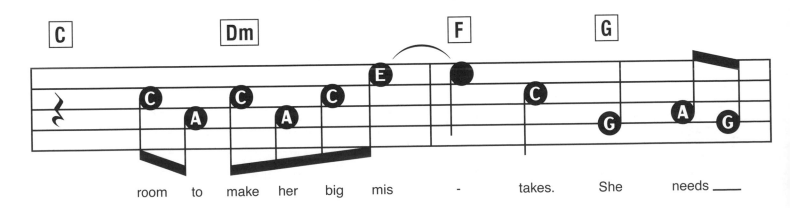

stood there and let her own folks know she need - ed

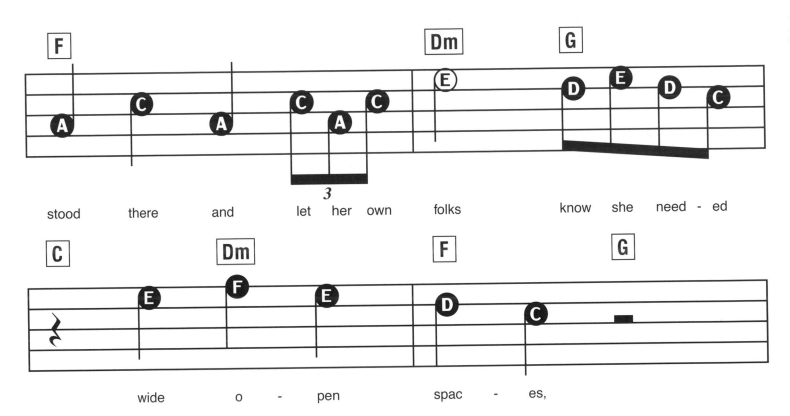

wide o - pen spac - es,

room to make her big mis - takes. She needs ____

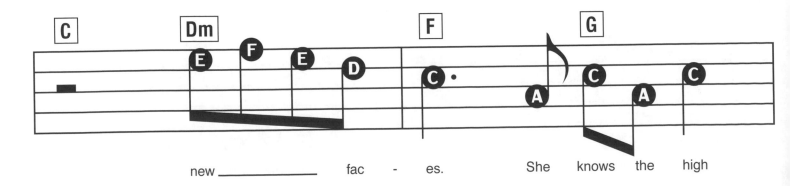

new ____ fac - es. She knows the high

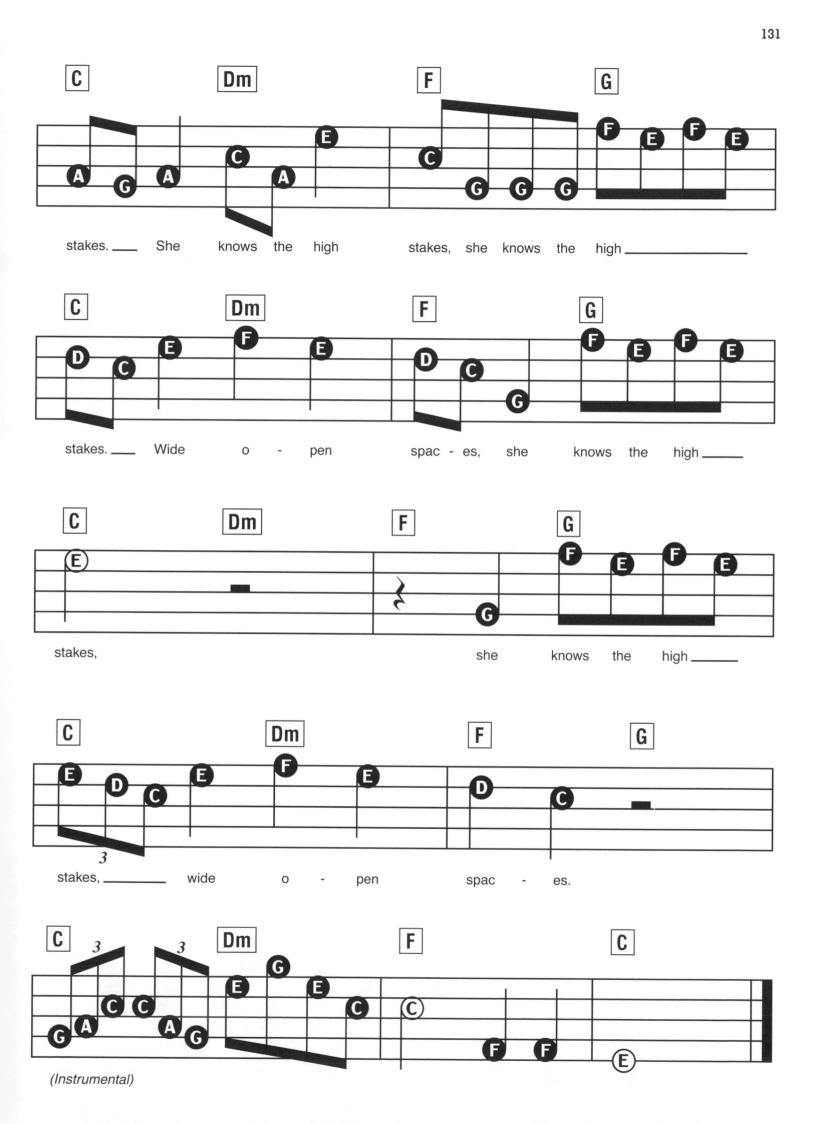

stakes. ___ She knows the high stakes, she knows the high _____

stakes. ___ Wide o - pen spac - es, she knows the high _____

stakes, she knows the high _____

stakes, _____ wide o - pen spac - es.

(Instrumental)

Your Man

Registration 1
Rhythm: Country Rock or 8-Beat

Words and Music by Jace Everett,
Chris DuBois and Chris Stapleton

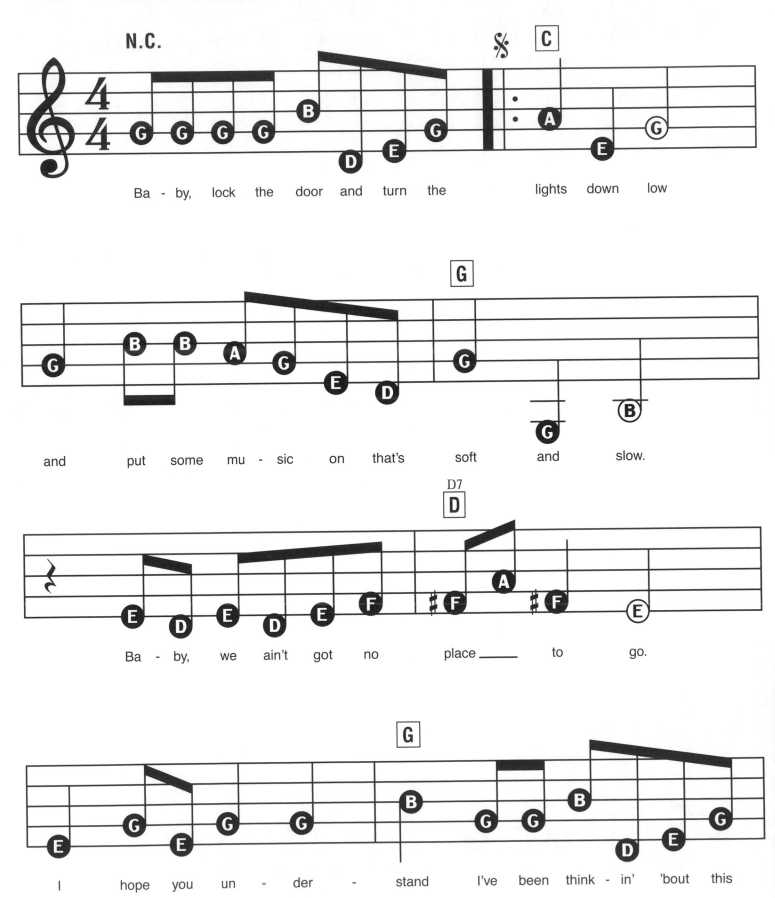

134

Registration Guide

- Match the Registration number on the song to the corresponding numbered category below. Select and activate an instrumental sound available on your instrument.

- Choose an automatic rhythm appropriate to the mood and style of the song. (Consult your Owner's Guide for proper operation of automatic rhythm features.)

- Adjust the tempo and volume controls to comfortable settings.

Registration

1	Mellow	Flutes, Clarinet, Oboe, Flugel Horn, Trombone, French Horn, Organ Flutes
2	Ensemble	Brass Section, Sax Section, Wind Ensemble, Full Organ, Theater Organ
3	Strings	Violin, Viola, Cello, Fiddle, String Ensemble, Pizzicato, Organ Strings
4	Guitars	Acoustic/Electric Guitars, Banjo, Mandolin, Dulcimer, Ukulele, Hawaiian Guitar
5	Mallets	Vibraphone, Marimba, Xylophone, Steel Drums, Bells, Celesta, Chimes
6	Liturgical	Pipe Organ, Hand Bells, Vocal Ensemble, Choir, Organ Flutes
7	Bright	Saxophones, Trumpet, Mute Trumpet, Synth Leads, Jazz/Gospel Organs
8	Piano	Piano, Electric Piano, Honky Tonk Piano, Harpsichord, Clavi
9	Novelty	Melodic Percussion, Wah Trumpet, Synth, Whistle, Kazoo, Perc. Organ
10	Bellows	Accordion, French Accordion, Mussette, Harmonica, Pump Organ, Bagpipes

E-Z PLAY® TODAY PUBLICATIONS

The E-Z Play® Today songbook series is the shortest distance between beginning music and playing fun! Check out this list of highlights and visit www.halleonard.com for a complete listing of all volumes and songlists.

<table>
<tr><td>00102278</td><td>1. Favorite Songs with 3 Chords</td><td>$7.95</td></tr>
<tr><td>00100374</td><td>2. Country Sound</td><td>$8.95</td></tr>
<tr><td>00100167</td><td>3. Contemporary Disney</td><td>$16.99</td></tr>
<tr><td>00100382</td><td>4. Dance Band Greats</td><td>$7.95</td></tr>
<tr><td>00100305</td><td>5. All-Time Standards</td><td>$7.99</td></tr>
<tr><td>00100428</td><td>6. Songs of The Beatles</td><td>$10.99</td></tr>
<tr><td>00100442</td><td>7. Hits from Musicals</td><td>$7.99</td></tr>
<tr><td>00100490</td><td>8. Patriotic Songs</td><td>$8.99</td></tr>
<tr><td>00100355</td><td>9. Christmas Time</td><td>$7.95</td></tr>
<tr><td>00100435</td><td>10. Hawaiian Songs</td><td>$7.95</td></tr>
<tr><td>00110284</td><td>12. Star Wars</td><td>$7.99</td></tr>
<tr><td>00100248</td><td>13. Three-Chord Country Songs</td><td>$12.95</td></tr>
<tr><td>00100300</td><td>14. All-Time Requests</td><td>$8.99</td></tr>
<tr><td>00100370</td><td>15. Country Pickin's</td><td>$7.95</td></tr>
<tr><td>00100335</td><td>16. Broadway's Best</td><td>$7.95</td></tr>
<tr><td>00100362</td><td>18. Classical Portraits</td><td>$7.99</td></tr>
<tr><td>00102277</td><td>20. Hymns</td><td>$7.95</td></tr>
<tr><td>00100570</td><td>22. Sacred Sounds</td><td>$7.95</td></tr>
<tr><td>00100214</td><td>23. Essential Songs – The 1920s</td><td>$16.95</td></tr>
<tr><td>00100206</td><td>24. Essential Songs – The 1930s</td><td>$16.95</td></tr>
<tr><td>14041364</td><td>26. Bob Dylan</td><td>$12.99</td></tr>
<tr><td>00001236</td><td>27. 60 of the World's Easiest to Play Songs with 3 Chords</td><td>$8.95</td></tr>
<tr><td>00101598</td><td>28. Fifty Classical Themes</td><td>$9.95</td></tr>
<tr><td>00100135</td><td>29. Love Songs</td><td>$7.95</td></tr>
<tr><td>00100030</td><td>30. Country Connection</td><td>$8.95</td></tr>
<tr><td>00001289</td><td>32. Sing-Along Favorites</td><td>$7.95</td></tr>
<tr><td>00100253</td><td>34. Inspirational Ballads</td><td>$10.95</td></tr>
<tr><td>00100254</td><td>35. Frank Sinatra – Romance</td><td>$8.95</td></tr>
<tr><td>00100122</td><td>36. Good Ol' Songs</td><td>$10.95</td></tr>
<tr><td>00100410</td><td>37. Favorite Latin Songs</td><td>$7.95</td></tr>
<tr><td>00119955</td><td>40. Coldplay</td><td>$10.99</td></tr>
<tr><td>00100425</td><td>41. Songs of Gershwin, Porter & Rodgers</td><td>$7.95</td></tr>
<tr><td>00100123</td><td>42. Baby Boomers Songbook</td><td>$9.95</td></tr>
<tr><td>00100576</td><td>43. Sing-along Requests</td><td>$8.95</td></tr>
<tr><td>00102135</td><td>44. Best of Willie Nelson</td><td>$9.99</td></tr>
<tr><td>00100460</td><td>45. Love Ballads</td><td>$8.99</td></tr>
<tr><td>00100007</td><td>47. Duke Ellington – American Composer</td><td>$8.95</td></tr>
<tr><td>00100343</td><td>48. Gospel Songs of Johnny Cash</td><td>$7.95</td></tr>
<tr><td>00100043</td><td>49. Elvis, Elvis, Elvis</td><td>$9.95</td></tr>
<tr><td>00102114</td><td>50. Best of Patsy Cline</td><td>$9.95</td></tr>
<tr><td>00100208</td><td>51. Essential Songs – The 1950s</td><td>$17.95</td></tr>
<tr><td>00100209</td><td>52. Essential Songs – The 1960s</td><td>$17.95</td></tr>
<tr><td>00100210</td><td>53. Essential Songs – The 1970s</td><td>$19.95</td></tr>
<tr><td>00100211</td><td>54. Essential Songs – The 1980s</td><td>$19.95</td></tr>
<tr><td>00100342</td><td>55. Johnny Cash</td><td>$9.99</td></tr>
<tr><td>00100118</td><td>57. More of the Best Songs Ever</td><td>$17.99</td></tr>
<tr><td>00100285</td><td>58. Four-Chord Songs</td><td>$10.99</td></tr>
<tr><td>00100353</td><td>59. Christmas Songs</td><td>$8.95</td></tr>
<tr><td>00100304</td><td>60. Songs for All Occasions</td><td>$16.99</td></tr>
<tr><td>00102314</td><td>61. Jazz Standards</td><td>$10.95</td></tr>
<tr><td>00100409</td><td>62. Favorite Hymns</td><td>$6.95</td></tr>
<tr><td>00100360</td><td>63. Classical Music (Spanish/English)</td><td>$7.99</td></tr>
<tr><td>00102223</td><td>64. Wicked</td><td>$9.95</td></tr>
<tr><td>00100217</td><td>65. Hymns with 3 Chords</td><td>$7.95</td></tr>
<tr><td>00102312</td><td>66. Torch Songs</td><td>$14.95</td></tr>
<tr><td>00100218</td><td>67. Music from the Motion Picture Ray</td><td>$8.95</td></tr>
<tr><td>00100449</td><td>69. It's Gospel</td><td>$7.95</td></tr>
<tr><td>00100432</td><td>70. Gospel Greats</td><td>$7.95</td></tr>
<tr><td>00100117</td><td>72. Canciones Románticas</td><td>$7.99</td></tr>
<tr><td>00100568</td><td>75. Sacred Moments</td><td>$6.95</td></tr>
<tr><td>00100572</td><td>76. The Sound of Music</td><td>$8.95</td></tr>
<tr><td>00100489</td><td>77. My Fair Lady</td><td>$7.99</td></tr>
<tr><td>00100424</td><td>81. Frankie Yankovic – Polkas & Waltzes</td><td>$7.95</td></tr>
<tr><td>00100286</td><td>87. 50 Worship Standards</td><td>$14.99</td></tr>
<tr><td>00102287</td><td>88. Glee</td><td>$9.99</td></tr>
<tr><td>00100577</td><td>89. Songs for Children</td><td>$7.95</td></tr>
<tr><td>00290104</td><td>90. Elton John Anthology</td><td>$16.99</td></tr>
<tr><td>00100034</td><td>91. 30 Songs for a Better World</td><td>$8.95</td></tr>
<tr><td>00100288</td><td>92. Michael Bublé – Crazy Love</td><td>$10.99</td></tr>
<tr><td>00100036</td><td>93. Country Hits</td><td>$10.95</td></tr>
<tr><td>00100139</td><td>94. Jim Croce – Greatest Hits</td><td>$8.95</td></tr>
<tr><td>00100219</td><td>95. The Phantom of the Opera (Movie)</td><td>$10.95</td></tr>
<tr><td>00100263</td><td>96. Mamma Mia – Movie Soundtrack</td><td>$7.99</td></tr>
<tr><td>00109768</td><td>98. Flower Power</td><td>$16.99</td></tr>
<tr><td>00100125</td><td>99. Children's Christmas Songs</td><td>$7.95</td></tr>
<tr><td>00100602</td><td>100. Winter Wonderland</td><td>$8.95</td></tr>
<tr><td>00001309</td><td>102. Carols of Christmas</td><td>$7.99</td></tr>
<tr><td>00119237</td><td>103. Two-Chord Songs</td><td>$9.99</td></tr>
</table>

<table>
<tr><td>00100256</td><td>107. The Best Praise & Worship Songs Ever</td><td>$16.99</td></tr>
<tr><td>00100363</td><td>108. Classical Themes (English/Spanish)</td><td>$6.95</td></tr>
<tr><td>00102232</td><td>109. Motown's Greatest Hits</td><td>$12.95</td></tr>
<tr><td>00101566</td><td>110. Neil Diamond Collection</td><td>$14.99</td></tr>
<tr><td>00100119</td><td>111. Season's Greetings</td><td>$14.95</td></tr>
<tr><td>00101498</td><td>112. Best of The Beatles</td><td>$19.95</td></tr>
<tr><td>00100134</td><td>114. Country Gospel USA</td><td>$10.95</td></tr>
<tr><td>00101612</td><td>115. The Greatest Waltzes</td><td>$9.95</td></tr>
<tr><td>00100136</td><td>118. 100 Kids' Songs</td><td>$12.95</td></tr>
<tr><td>00100433</td><td>120. Gospel of Bill & Gloria Gaither</td><td>$14.95</td></tr>
<tr><td>00100333</td><td>121. Boogies, Blues and Rags</td><td>$7.95</td></tr>
<tr><td>00100146</td><td>122. Songs for Praise & Worship</td><td>$8.95</td></tr>
<tr><td>00100001</td><td>125. Great Big Book of Children's Songs</td><td>$14.99</td></tr>
<tr><td>00101563</td><td>127. John Denver's Greatest Hits</td><td>$9.95</td></tr>
<tr><td>00116947</td><td>128. John Williams</td><td>$10.99</td></tr>
<tr><td>00116956</td><td>130. Taylor Swift Hits</td><td>$10.99</td></tr>
<tr><td>00102318</td><td>131. Doo-Wop Songbook</td><td>$10.95</td></tr>
<tr><td>00100306</td><td>133. Carole King</td><td>$9.99</td></tr>
<tr><td>00100171</td><td>135. All Around the U.S.A.</td><td>$10.95</td></tr>
<tr><td>00001256</td><td>136. Christmas Is for Kids</td><td>$8.99</td></tr>
<tr><td>00100144</td><td>137. Children's Movie Hits</td><td>$7.95</td></tr>
<tr><td>00100038</td><td>138. Nostalgia Collection</td><td>$14.95</td></tr>
<tr><td>00100289</td><td>139. Crooners</td><td>$19.99</td></tr>
<tr><td>00101956</td><td>140. Best of George Strait</td><td>$12.95</td></tr>
<tr><td>00100314</td><td>142. Classic Jazz</td><td>$14.99</td></tr>
<tr><td>00101946</td><td>143. The Songs of Paul McCartney</td><td>$8.99</td></tr>
<tr><td>00100597</td><td>146. Hank Williams – His Best</td><td>$7.95</td></tr>
<tr><td>00116916</td><td>147. Lincoln</td><td>$7.99</td></tr>
<tr><td>00100003</td><td>149. Movie Musical Memories</td><td>$10.95</td></tr>
<tr><td>00101548</td><td>150. Best Big Band Songs Ever</td><td>$16.95</td></tr>
<tr><td>00100152</td><td>151. Beach Boys – Greatest Hits</td><td>$8.95</td></tr>
<tr><td>00101592</td><td>152. Fiddler on the Roof</td><td>$9.99</td></tr>
<tr><td>00101549</td><td>155. Best of Billy Joel</td><td>$10.99</td></tr>
<tr><td>00001264</td><td>157. Easy Favorites</td><td>$7.99</td></tr>
<tr><td>00100315</td><td>160. The Grammy Awards Record of the Year 1958-2010</td><td>$16.99</td></tr>
<tr><td>00100293</td><td>161. Henry Mancini</td><td>$9.99</td></tr>
<tr><td>00100049</td><td>162. Lounge Music</td><td>$10.95</td></tr>
<tr><td>00100295</td><td>163. The Very Best of the Rat Pack</td><td>$12.99</td></tr>
<tr><td>00101530</td><td>164. Best Christmas Songbook</td><td>$9.95</td></tr>
<tr><td>00101895</td><td>165. Rodgers & Hammerstein Songbook</td><td>$9.95</td></tr>
<tr><td>00100148</td><td>169. A Charlie Brown Christmas™</td><td>$10.99</td></tr>
<tr><td>00101900</td><td>170. Kenny Rogers – Greatest Hits</td><td>$9.95</td></tr>
<tr><td>00101537</td><td>171. Best of Elton John</td><td>$7.95</td></tr>
<tr><td>00100321</td><td>173. Adele – 21</td><td>$10.99</td></tr>
<tr><td>00100149</td><td>176. Charlie Brown Collection™</td><td>$7.99</td></tr>
<tr><td>00102325</td><td>179. Love Songs of The Beatles</td><td>$10.99</td></tr>
<tr><td>00101610</td><td>181. Great American Country Songbook</td><td>$12.95</td></tr>
<tr><td>00001246</td><td>182. Amazing Grace</td><td>$12.95</td></tr>
<tr><td>00450133</td><td>183. West Side Story</td><td>$9.99</td></tr>
<tr><td>00100151</td><td>185. Carpenters</td><td>$10.99</td></tr>
<tr><td>00101606</td><td>186. 40 Pop & Rock Song Classics</td><td>$12.95</td></tr>
<tr><td>00100155</td><td>187. Ultimate Christmas</td><td>$17.95</td></tr>
<tr><td>00102276</td><td>189. Irish Favorites</td><td>$7.95</td></tr>
<tr><td>00100053</td><td>191. Jazz Love Songs</td><td>$8.95</td></tr>
<tr><td>00101998</td><td>192. 65 Standard Hits</td><td>$15.95</td></tr>
<tr><td>00123123</td><td>193. Bruno Mars</td><td>$10.99</td></tr>
<tr><td>00124609</td><td>195. Opera Favorites</td><td>$8.99</td></tr>
<tr><td>00101609</td><td>196. Best of George Gershwin</td><td>$14.99</td></tr>
<tr><td>00100057</td><td>198. Songs in 3/4 Time</td><td>$9.95</td></tr>
<tr><td>00119857</td><td>199. Jumbo Songbook</td><td>$24.99</td></tr>
<tr><td>00101539</td><td>200. Best Songs Ever</td><td>$19.95</td></tr>
<tr><td>00101540</td><td>202. Best Country Songs Ever</td><td>$17.95</td></tr>
<tr><td>00101541</td><td>203. Best Broadway Songs Ever</td><td>$17.99</td></tr>
<tr><td>00101542</td><td>204. Best Easy Listening Songs Ever</td><td>$17.95</td></tr>
<tr><td>00101543</td><td>205. Best Love Songs Ever</td><td>$17.95</td></tr>
<tr><td>00100058</td><td>208. Easy Listening Favorites</td><td>$7.95</td></tr>
<tr><td>00100059</td><td>210. '60s Pop Rock Hits</td><td>$12.95</td></tr>
<tr><td>14041777</td><td>211. The Big Book of Nursery Rhymes & Children's Songs</td><td>$12.99</td></tr>
<tr><td>00126895</td><td>212. Frozen</td><td>$9.99</td></tr>
<tr><td>00101546</td><td>213. Disney Classics</td><td>$14.95</td></tr>
<tr><td>00101533</td><td>215. Best Christmas Songs Ever</td><td>$19.95</td></tr>
<tr><td>00100156</td><td>219. Christmas Songs with 3 Chords</td><td>$8.99</td></tr>
<tr><td>00102080</td><td>225. Lawrence Welk Songbook</td><td>$9.95</td></tr>
<tr><td>00101931</td><td>228. Songs of the '20s</td><td>$13.95</td></tr>
<tr><td>00101932</td><td>229. Songs of the '30s</td><td>$13.95</td></tr>
<tr><td>00101933</td><td>230. Songs of the '40s</td><td>$14.95</td></tr>
</table>

<table>
<tr><td>00101935</td><td>232. Songs of the '60s</td><td>$14.95</td></tr>
<tr><td>00101936</td><td>233. Songs of the '70s</td><td>$14.95</td></tr>
<tr><td>00101581</td><td>235. Elvis Presley Anthology</td><td>$15.99</td></tr>
<tr><td>00290170</td><td>239. Big Book of Children's Songs</td><td>$14.95</td></tr>
<tr><td>00290120</td><td>240. Frank Sinatra</td><td>$14.95</td></tr>
<tr><td>00100158</td><td>243. Oldies! Oldies! Oldies!</td><td>$10.95</td></tr>
<tr><td>00290242</td><td>244. Songs of the '80s</td><td>$14.95</td></tr>
<tr><td>00100041</td><td>245. Best of Simon & Garfunkel</td><td>$8.95</td></tr>
<tr><td>00100269</td><td>247. Essential Songs – Broadway</td><td>$17.99</td></tr>
<tr><td>00100296</td><td>248. The Love Songs of Elton John</td><td>$12.99</td></tr>
<tr><td>00100175</td><td>249. Elvis – 30 #1 Hits</td><td>$9.95</td></tr>
<tr><td>00102113</td><td>251. Phantom of the Opera (Broadway)</td><td>$14.95</td></tr>
<tr><td>00100301</td><td>255. Four-Chord Hymns</td><td>$8.99</td></tr>
<tr><td>00100203</td><td>256. Very Best of Lionel Richie</td><td>$8.95</td></tr>
<tr><td>00100302</td><td>258. Four-Chord Worship</td><td>$9.99</td></tr>
<tr><td>00100178</td><td>259. Norah Jones – Come Away with Me</td><td>$9.95</td></tr>
<tr><td>00102306</td><td>261. Best of Andrew Lloyd Webber</td><td>$12.95</td></tr>
<tr><td>00100063</td><td>266. Latin Hits</td><td>$7.95</td></tr>
<tr><td>00100062</td><td>269. Love That Latin Beat</td><td>$7.95</td></tr>
<tr><td>00100179</td><td>270. Christian Christmas Songbook</td><td>$14.95</td></tr>
<tr><td>00101425</td><td>272. ABBA Gold – Greatest Hits</td><td>$7.95</td></tr>
<tr><td>00102248</td><td>275. Classical Hits – Bach, Beethoven & Brahms</td><td>$6.95</td></tr>
<tr><td>00100186</td><td>277. Stevie Wonder – Greatest Hits</td><td>$9.95</td></tr>
<tr><td>00100237</td><td>280. Dolly Parton</td><td>$9.99</td></tr>
<tr><td>00100068</td><td>283. Best Jazz Standards Ever</td><td>$15.95</td></tr>
<tr><td>00100244</td><td>287. Josh Groban</td><td>$10.95</td></tr>
<tr><td>00100022</td><td>288. Sing-a-Long Christmas</td><td>$10.95</td></tr>
<tr><td>00100023</td><td>289. Sing-a-Long Christmas Carols</td><td>$9.95</td></tr>
<tr><td>00102124</td><td>293. Movie Classics</td><td>$9.95</td></tr>
<tr><td>00100069</td><td>294. Old Fashioned Love Songs</td><td>$9.95</td></tr>
<tr><td>00100303</td><td>295. Best of Michael Bublé</td><td>$12.99</td></tr>
<tr><td>00100075</td><td>296. Best of Cole Porter</td><td>$7.95</td></tr>
<tr><td>00102130</td><td>298. Beautiful Love Songs</td><td>$7.95</td></tr>
<tr><td>00001102</td><td>301. Kid's Songfest</td><td>$9.99</td></tr>
<tr><td>00102147</td><td>306. Irving Berlin Collection</td><td>$14.95</td></tr>
<tr><td>00102182</td><td>308. Greatest American Songbook</td><td>$9.99</td></tr>
<tr><td>00100194</td><td>309. 3-Chord Rock 'n' Roll</td><td>$8.95</td></tr>
<tr><td>00001580</td><td>311. The Platters Anthology</td><td>$7.95</td></tr>
<tr><td>02501515</td><td>312. Barbra – Love Is the Answer</td><td>$10.99</td></tr>
<tr><td>00100196</td><td>314. Chicago</td><td>$8.95</td></tr>
<tr><td>00100197</td><td>315. VH1's 100 Greatest Songs of Rock & Roll</td><td>$19.95</td></tr>
<tr><td>00100080</td><td>322. Dixieland</td><td>$7.95</td></tr>
<tr><td>00100277</td><td>325. Taylor Swift</td><td>$10.99</td></tr>
<tr><td>00100082</td><td>327. Tonight at the Lounge</td><td>$7.95</td></tr>
<tr><td>00100092</td><td>333. Great Gospel Favorites</td><td>$7.95</td></tr>
<tr><td>00100278</td><td>338. The Best Hymns Ever</td><td>$19.99</td></tr>
<tr><td>00100279</td><td>340. Anthology of Jazz Songs</td><td>$19.99</td></tr>
<tr><td>00100280</td><td>341. Anthology of Rock Songs</td><td>$19.99</td></tr>
<tr><td>00100281</td><td>342. Anthology of Broadway Songs</td><td>$19.99</td></tr>
<tr><td>00100282</td><td>343. Anthology of Love Songs</td><td>$19.99</td></tr>
<tr><td>00100283</td><td>344. Anthology of Latin Songs</td><td>$19.99</td></tr>
<tr><td>00100284</td><td>345. Anthology of Movie Songs</td><td>$19.99</td></tr>
<tr><td>00102235</td><td>346. Big Book of Christmas Songs</td><td>$14.95</td></tr>
<tr><td>00100292</td><td>347. Anthology of Country Songs</td><td>$19.99</td></tr>
<tr><td>00100095</td><td>359. 100 Years of Song</td><td>$17.95</td></tr>
<tr><td>00100096</td><td>360. More 100 Years of Song</td><td>$19.95</td></tr>
<tr><td>00100103</td><td>375. Songs of Bacharach & David</td><td>$7.95</td></tr>
<tr><td>00100107</td><td>392. Disney Favorites</td><td>$19.95</td></tr>
<tr><td>00100108</td><td>393. Italian Favorites</td><td>$7.95</td></tr>
<tr><td>00100111</td><td>394. Best Gospel Songs Ever</td><td>$17.95</td></tr>
<tr><td>00100114</td><td>398. Disney's Princess Collections</td><td>$10.99</td></tr>
<tr><td>00100115</td><td>400. Classical Masterpieces</td><td>$10.95</td></tr>
</table>

HAL•LEONARD® CORPORATION

7777 W. BLUEMOUND RD. P.O. BOX 13819 MILWAUKEE, WI 53213

Prices, contents, and availability subject to change without notice.

0714